Holistic Success

Other Books by Robert Puff, Ph.D.

Reflections on Meditation: A Guide for Beginners
Success Beyond Your Imagination: Working in the Zone
Holistic Health
Getting it Right: A Guide to Healthy Relationships
How to Live a Positive Life
Living a Peaceful Life
Meditation for Health and Happiness
Raising Healthy Children and Teenagers
Spiritual Enlightenment: Awakening to the Supreme Reality
Anger Work: How to Express Your Anger and Still Be Kind

Visit www.doctorpuff.com for more!

Other Books by Kristen M. White, Psy.D.

R u red-e 4 conflict? Speaking Human in the Digital Age
Diet Free Forever: Level I – Mindful Eating (Audio Series & Workbook)
Diet Free Forever: Level II – Emotional Eating (Audio Series & Workbook)
Diet Free Forever: Level I – Obstacles to Health (Audio Series & Workbook)

Visit www.kristenmwhite.com for more!

Holistic Success: How to Dance Through Life with the Abandon of a Child and the Skill of a Master

by
Robert Puff, Ph.D. &
Kristen M. White, Psy.D.

Robert Puff, Ph.D.
2436 West Coast Highway #103
Newport Beach, CA 92663
Tel: (714) 337-4889
www.doctorpuff.com

Ordering Information
Quantity Sales. We provide discounts for bulk purchases by certain organizations. For details, contact us.
Individual Sales. Robert Puff publications are available through most bookstores, online and off, and on his website at www.doctorpuff.com

Printed in the United States of America
ISBN-13: 978-1482310863
ISBN-10: 1482310864

To all those who are seeking a holistic, healthy, and happy life…even when this means going against the grain. And to all who have helped us to get there.

Contents

Introduction

Sometimes it feels like we have two left feet. We step out onto the dance floor, hoping we are ready to move around the floor with ease and grace…only to end up stepping on our partners' toes or dancing completely out-of-sync with the music and the rest of the group. We may lack skill, coordination, or even balance. Whatever the reason, our dancing is stilted and off—at best creating a little embarrassment, at worst causing us to knock over the dancers (or even furniture!) around us.

If it's just dancing, we can probably handle it by avoiding the party—or at least the dance floor. But what if we have two left feet *in life*? What if, despite our best intentions and efforts, we seem to move through life in much the same way—stepping on our partners' toes, getting off-beat, embarrassing ourselves, and perhaps even creating disaster in our wake? We can't very well avoid the party of life, and we probably don't want to live out our days sipping drinks, alone, in the corner of the room. Having two left feet in life is a little more problematic.

And yet, many, many people experience having two left feet in life. Sometimes it's just in one area—maybe they dance with grace and ease at work, but they constantly step on their partner's (or kids' or friends') toes at home. Alternatively, maybe they are in perfect sync with their partners, but they seem to be leaving a disaster in their wake financially. For other people, it's all of these areas and more. Some people seem to have two left feet throughout life—stepping on people's toes relationally, feeling off-beat professionally or emotionally, knowing they are out-of-shape mentally and physically, *and* leaving disaster behind them financially. Phew! What then? Whether we have two left feet in one area or many, must we then avoid the dance floor of life?

Dancing with Ease and Grace

Not at all! The good news today is we can learn to dance with ease, grace, and fluidity through all areas of life. We can actually replace the laborious, boring, and even stressful ways we usually stumble clumsily from alarm clock to exhaustion through our days. In fact, we can trade in those two left feet for the skilled, smooth movements of an expert dancer. In addition, we can trade in those two, worn down, tired feet for the spontaneity, playfulness, freedom, and all-out-abandon of a dancing child. Yes, that's right—dancing with ease and grace through life combines the skill of a master and the abandon of a free-spirited child.

Let's look a little more at the master first. The master is an expert dancer. He's learned and honed how to move everything from his feet to his hips, staying in sync with the music and his partner(s). In other words, he's *really* good at his craft. In life, this means that he's *really* good at living. He knows how to keep his body in shape and deal with difficult emotions or circumstances when they arise. He also has thriving, intimate relationships with all sorts of people. What's more, he has a job he truly enjoys and stability in his finances. In other words, he's good at living. Yes, that's right—he's not just good at work or staying in shape; this holistically successful man clearly has skill on the dance floor of life.

What's more, he *enjoys* living. And for this, it's not enough to simply be a skilled dancer. Simply imagine a dancer who knows the right moves but engages them without any passion. The dance would probably look rather flat and stale. Dancers look better when they put their whole heart and soul into the moment, feeling the song and enjoying the movement. In this sense, dancers are at their best when they are like a little four-year-old, moving her body freely to the music. She's spontaneous, playful, and full of abandon. She's not worried about how she looks or whether she's doing it right—she's simply enjoying the moment. It behooves us to also learn a thing or two from this child, thus enabling us to infuse our dance through life with pleasure, life, and vitality.

Hence, dancing with ease, grace, and fluidity through life combines the skill of the master with the abandon of the child. In fact, it involves being so skilled that the moves become second nature; then we can throw up our arms like the free-spirited child and simply spin in crazy, glorious circles. In life, this means that we can look great and have fantastic results…without feeling like we are working hard all the time. We can actually move with a combination of great skill and utter, free-spirited enjoyment.

Preparing for the Number Ahead

So this all sounds great, but how do we actually trade in our two, left, tired feet for the talented, free-spirited feet in the dance of life? First of all, we have to learn new skills. We know this instinctively if we are thinking about starting or improving upon a job or hobby. In order to be good at it, we have to learn and refine our skills. For example, if we want to learn to play tennis or even just improve our game, we take lessons, acquiring new skills and honing other ones in everything from our serve to our backhand. Although this is obvious with tennis, we often think (or at least act like) these skills should just come naturally in life. We believe that we should just know how to communicate well with others, even during conflict. We act like we'll simply "fall into" a career we love and automatically find success. And, of course, handling our emotions will come easily no matter what life throws our way. Right?? As we discover when life starts to go amiss, this really isn't the case. Just like any job or hobby, we often have to learn and hone our life skills too.

Of course, it isn't enough to just know *about* something. We could learn all about tennis swings out of a book or via the internet, without actually improving our game at all. Why? Because it's different to know something in our head and to know it in our lives. In order to acquire new life skills, we have to learn about them and *practice* them. Yes, that's right, we said *practice*. Unlike most books, this one is not here to just provide information. We will provide a lot of great information, but we know that getting results—in a sport, job, or life skill—requires application and practice. The expert dancer both learns and practices, and so shall we.

As we said, though, we don't want to become skilled experts without heart. Like the child, we want to *enjoy* the dance of life, moment-by-moment along the way. The fact of the matter is that it is good to seek mastery, but true happiness and holistic success require us to be present now. It turns out that the *process* is as important as the *destination*, and being good at life doesn't necessarily mean doing it perfectly all the time. Instead, we must learn to balance our strivings for mastery with the ability to simply enjoy the journey today. Like that child dancing with abandon, being able to *engage fully in the present moment* allows us to experience and enjoy now, infusing our life with pleasure, life, and vitality.

As a result, this book does two things. First, it combines information and practice about developing the skills of a master. Yes, we'll provide both information about each important area *and* opportunities to truly practice them so that we can truly become skilled masters. Second, this book also provides information and practice on learning to enjoy life right where we're at by simply being present in today; then we can also gain that abandon of the child. More specifically, this book will integrate these two areas of skill and presence into specific tips for success in life, covering everything from the body and mind to work and relationships. Why all of these areas? Because we believe that one secret to true happiness and success is a holistic focus. Hence, we'll start with holistic health and then move through each of the most important areas in our lives, offering concrete ways to master and enjoy each one. We'll offer an overview and three specific tips for each area, making eighteen tips total. These tips are not exhaustive, but they do include all of our top tips for holistic success—the success of dancing through life with abandon, skill, and ease.

Getting to Know Your Partners

As we start on this journey together, you may be wondering who you are dancing with...and perhaps even why. Why become partners with us versus someone else? There are two reasons really. First of all, we're both practicing, clinical psychologists. In other words, we're trained experts in helping people to live well. We literally have doctorates that aid us in understanding everything from how to deal with difficult emotions to how to communicate well with our partners. What's more, we spend our days helping people apply all this knowledge in their lives. As a result, what's written in this book isn't some random theory we thought up one day—it's well-founded, often even researched ideas that have already helped real people find greater holistic success in their lives.

That leads us to the second reason to partner with us: We understand this journey personally. Both of us grew up in loving, well-meaning families who unintentionally left us a lot of deficits in the skills of living when we got to adulthood. In spite of our best efforts and intentions, we struggled with emotions, relationships, the body, and more. We were still "successful" in terms of degrees and achievements, but we had some pretty unhappy seasons in life. Neither of us were very good at just accepting that as the status quo, so we did everything we could think of to get some answers and find some change—traveling the world, reading classics and gurus, going back to school, even entering into our own therapy. These journeys allowed us to learn about emotions, people, life, and—perhaps most importantly—ourselves.

And the results? We both found greater happiness and success in our own lives—holistically. For Dr. White, this meant moving from being perpetually single, lonely, stressed, bored, and obese to a place of getting fit, enjoying life with an awesome husband, and finding a career that nourishes her soul. For Dr. Puff, it meant going from the over-worked tasks of a depressed achiever to the settled joys of a family-man who is fully present with life and has a fulfilling career to provide abundantly for his family. Truly, our journeys resulted in a degree of holistic success that we never even dreamed possible before.

Most amazingly though, life simply has a different quality to it now. Before, it felt kind of like mountain climbing. We were constantly pushing ourselves uphill, trying to reach the next achievement and crest that next summit…which always seemed to be followed by another summit to climb. Like a mountain climber constantly going uphill, life was full of hard work and struggle, yet without the needed reward or rest for all of that effort.

Now, life holds the ease, joy, and beauty of those dancers. We work hard, yet we truly have a sense of enjoyment, peace, purpose, and hope that was not there before.

Our personal journeys and changes are what led each of us to become psychologists. They're also what encouraged us to take what we know out of the therapy office and the classroom. Through our writing and speaking, we hope to share the secrets we've learned about living well and enjoying life with "normal" people in all avenues of life. Truly, we have a passion for helping others find the holistic happiness and success they really want in life. We know it's possible because we've both walked the journey ourselves and helped many other people along their way.

Dancing Starts Now!

Now, we'd like to help you. We want to share all that we've learned, both personally and professionally, to help you dance with greater ease, fluidity, and grace through life. We want to enable you to trade in your two, tired, left feet—whether in one area or throughout life—for those skilled feet of the master and carefree ones of the child. Whether life is good and you want it to be great, or life is awful and you need a complete make-over, this book is about helping you to get better at living so that you can experience greater holistic success and enjoyment throughout life.

Clearly, this book is not a magic wand or a cure-all panacea. It's just a book. It's not going to instantly solve all your problems. It can't get you that job you need, make your kids behave or your mother-in-law move out, nor fix whatever other circumstances are tough in your life right now. Unfortunately, it's also not going to stave off future problems or difficulties. We will always have moments that are hard and circumstances that are difficult. However, we can have a greater sense of happiness and success—whether we are in the middle of ease and joy *or* difficulty and pain. We can have this happiness and success through accumulating certain skills in life and employing them in a holistic, engaged way.

Sound simple? Perhaps, but then moving with the ease, grace, and fluidity of a dancer usually sounds simple too…in theory. And, in fact, most of these ideas about living well in a holistically balanced, present-oriented way aren't rocket science. Many people have heard and talked about them before. However, that doesn't mean that we live this way. The truth is that many of us are still caught up in climbing that one last mountain, stating we'll slow down once we "arrive" to that last crest. Clearly, living consistently with the ease of a dancer, abandon of a child, and skill of a master requires something new and different. Interested? Then let's start dancing now!

Part I: Tips for Holistic Success

To be a really great dancer, it's not enough to master only one area or one set of moves. For dancers to move with grace, they have to know how to move their feet, hips, arms, and every other part of their body. The best dancers actually know how to move all parts of their bodies in many different types of dance too. They're also able to rhythmically attend to the music and their partners. This combination of moving each part of the body well, attending to the music, and connecting with one's partner is required for true grace and success in dancing. Simply imagine a dancer who could move but had no sense of rhythm with the music or connection to his or her partner…the dance would not be graceful or beautiful, no matter how much talent the dancer possessed. Dancers are able to move with grace as they holistically attend to all pieces of the dance.

Similarly, if we want to move through life with the grace of a dancer, *we have to attend to all important areas of our lives.* This may include our work, relationships, bodies, hearts, minds, and spirituality. It's not enough to simply focus on one of these areas and expect to find overall happiness and success. Simply imagine the "successful" businessman who works 80 hours a week, running a viable company and making lots of money…while his marriage is on the rocks and his kids are having all kinds of problems at home or school. Like the dancer, it may take some effort and intentionality to attend to all important areas, yet this sort of holistic focus and balance is what creates overall grace and success as we dance through life.

While it's tempting and pretty normal to live in an imbalanced way, the truth is that very few (if any) of us find real, lasting happiness or peace narrowly focusing on one area of our lives. We simply aren't this segmented as people. Consider, for example, the life of Marilyn Monroe. Although she died in 1962, Marilyn Monroe remains to this day a pop icon and a symbol of femininity and beauty. She achieved incredible success during her life as an actress, singer, and model. In spite of this amazing professional success, however, Monroe hugely struggled in her personal life. During her childhood years, she vacillated between the care of her mentally ill mother and a number of foster homes. While she initially claimed she'd found happiness through her "Cinderella" success story as an adult, in actuality she was married and divorced three times and died of an apparent drug overdose at the young age of 36. Why did such stellar professional success not override her personal struggles to create happiness and peace? Because we are holistic beings.

Each area of us and our lives matters. Each area also impacts the others as well as our overall health. Even if we have a narrow goal, like being the best mom in the world, we'll fail if we only focus on parenting. Why?

Because our heart will give out from the poor care we've taken of our bodies, or perhaps we'll lose our house due to our financial ineptitude, interfering in huge ways with really providing the life we wanted for our kids. Whether we like it or not, we are holistic beings. True, lasting happiness and success in life require that we attend to all areas.

Before we begin discussing each of the specific, important areas of our lives, then, we must look at how to live holistically balanced and healthy lives in general. Hence, this section will provide three tips for living holistically. Each of these tips can be applied to overall living as well as each of the specific areas to come. In this way, holistic living provides a framework and structure for the rest of living.

Tip #1: Take in the Whole Picture

Imagine a painting of a small town in France. It's evening and the stars and moon shine brightly. A small range of mountains provides a backdrop for the town off to the right, and a large cypress tree stands in front of it on the left. Can you picture it? Does it look anything like Van Gogh's painting, "The Starry Night"? Ours doesn't! In spite of the fact that this is actually a description of Van Gogh's most famous work, the description of its details does not necessarily bring the painting to mind.

Why not? The reality is that what stands out to us about Van Gogh's painting is not the details. In fact, some of the details, such as the cypress tree, may even be surprising to us. What makes Van Gogh's painting unique and memorable is the swirly lines, soothing colors, and the way the whole scene flows together. If we were to look at only one or two details, we would miss the beauty…and perhaps even walk away unsure of what we were seeing. To really grasp the significance and beauty of Van Gogh's work, we must take in the whole picture.

Life is a lot like Van Gogh's painting. To focus on only one or two details is likely to leave us unimpressed and perhaps even confused. Simply imagine the man who focuses exclusively on his work, or the woman who only thinks about her kids. While these specific areas might flourish, these people are unlikely to find significance or beauty in the whole of their lives. As with Van Gogh's "Starry Night," we must take in the whole picture of life in order to really find the significance, beauty, and success we are seeking.

Holistic Integration

The truth is that we are whole people. We have many parts to us and our lives, such as our bodies, minds, hearts, relationships, work, and finances. Each of these parts is important and interdependent with the rest. Our emotions impact our bodies, which impact our relationships, which impact our work, which impacts our finances, which impact our stress level, which impacts our body…and on and on we go! Each part is important in its own right as well as for how it connects to the other parts of us and our lives.

In this vein, we're kind of like cars. Simply turning a car on requires us to utilize the key, ignition, brake, accelerator, gear shaft, and steering wheel. If any one of these parts fails to work properly, the car will not work as it was intended—it will not take us, for example, from our work to our home. None of us question that every part must be working properly for the car to run.

We, as human beings, are much more complex and intricately made than cars, yet we tend to doubt that we are as holistic or interconnected. We pretend that each part works in isolation of the others. We are often astounded when our stress creates knots in our backs or our frustration leads to stomachaches. We are sometimes even surprised when a fight with our partner makes it difficult to focus at work that day. We buy into the myth that everything we are and do works in isolation. In reality, we are interdependent systems in which each part impacts the other parts.

This holistic idea is not new. Although the phrase "holistic health" was not coined until 1926, it is an ancient idea. For centuries, it has emphasized our need for mind *and* body wellness. In modern, Western traditions, it often refers to the connection between physical illness and mental, emotional, and spiritual health. As we use it, holistic health refers to our need for wellness in all areas of our lives and beings. It's about attending to *all* of the various, important parts of us, as well as incorporating them into an integrated whole.

5 Key Areas

There are five key areas of ourselves and our lives to consider in holistic health and wellness. First, we have our bodies. Our bodies are the physical manifestation of our presence in the world. They contain everything from the beating of our hearts to the repeated firings of the neural pathways in our brains. As you probably already know, it is important for us to take care of our bodies through eating proper foods, exercising, and resting. All of these fundamental areas relate to the care of our physical bodies.

Second, we have our minds. Our minds can be conceived of as the source of our thoughts. These thoughts may be about ourselves, others, or life and the world in general. They often convey specific perspectives and attitudes as well—some positive, such as when we are proud of the things we've accomplished, and some negative, like when we are critical of other's failures. Equally important, our thoughts and attitudes tend to have a specific activity level; some people's minds run and on, perhaps offering a running commentary that keeps them up at night, while others have quieter minds. All of these components—from the specific content of our thoughts to the attitude they convey and activity level they possess—are integral pieces of the workings of the mind.

In addition to a mind and a body, we all have a heart or soul. Regardless of the word we use to describe this aspect of our being, it incorporates our emotions, allowing us to feel in response to life and simply play and enjoy things. Our heart also includes our spirituality or faith in something greater than ourselves. If our bodies are the frame for our being and our thoughts are perhaps the content, then our hearts would add the color and depth.

The three main areas that we've described so far—our bodies, minds, and hearts—are all internal; of course, we also know there are a variety of external influences in our lives. This brings us to our fourth area, which is work. Work is especially important because we tend to spend the bulk of our time there. This is also where we generate our money, which is a closely related and equally critical area. Both our work and our finances are huge areas of our lives.

The fifth key area in our lives is our relationships. Our relationships encompass our friends, family, partners, children, and even co-workers. With each of these groups, we have certain ways that we communicate and set boundaries. We also have a certain level of intimacy and vulnerability in each of these relationships. All of these pieces impact whether our relationships are healthy and satisfying.

Although there are undoubtedly other areas we could touch upon, these five areas make up a critical core for our lives. Our bodies, minds, and hearts represent the largely internal pieces that make up who we are as individuals. They determine how we interact with the external world, especially our work and relationships; then, in turn, they impact the internal aspects of us once again. Truly, all five of these areas are critical and interdependent in determining our happiness and success in life.

The Danger of Myopic Living

While we know that all five of these areas are important, it's often hard to live with them all in view. It's much easier to focus myopically on one or two areas of our lives to the near exclusion of all others. This was one of our biggest downfalls in the earlier parts of our lives. We focused exclusively on achieving professionally and were sadly lacking in relational intimacy, physical health, emotional health, and more. Like many others, our myopic focus created a deficit in many areas of our lives.

Dr. Puff: "While myopic living is actually pretty common, I see it most pointedly in my practice in Newport Beach. I regularly work with people who are exceedingly successful professionally and monetarily. They seem to have achieved what so many of us labor after day in and day out—nice cars, beautiful homes, great schools for their kids, the latest fashions, respect from those around them, etc., etc. In actual fact, however, many of these people come to my office with depression, anxiety, alcoholism, and other ailments. Sadly, this is not simply because successful people have their share of problems like the rest of us. It's often as much or more related to the fact that the wonderful professional and financial success they've achieved has taken so much of their time and attention that they've ignored other things, like their spouses, kids, or physical health. Now those "other things" are falling apart. Perhaps their spouse has left them or their kids are getting into major trouble. Maybe their doctors have told them that their lives are threatened by hypertension or other physical issues. Whatever the circumstances, their myopic living has taken a toll."

These "successful" but ailing people Dr. Puff mentions have mistakenly bought the idea that humans consist of a number of unrelated systems (e.g., mind, body, heart); as a result, they can thus pick and choose what's important to them. In reality, all parts of us are inter-related and interdependent. Over-focusing on one area may bring short-term success, but it's likely to cost us and make the journey much more difficult in the end. This is why holistic health refers to our need for holistic, integrated wellness in all five, key areas of our lives.

B's Mean Balance

Attending to all five of the critical areas requires balance. Balance is a pretty self-explanatory idea. Simply imagine two children balancing on a teeter totter or two sides of a scale hanging at equal heights—these pictures should remind you of what balance looks like. Balance involves paying attention to and funneling equal resources to multiple areas at once. While this may create tension between the different areas, balance is simple in theory.

As we know, however, balance is not always simple in our day-to-day lives. We have a limited amount of resources and it's hard to figure out how to funnel them appropriately. It just never seems like there's enough. As a result, it often turns out that certain areas, like our work, win out over other areas time and again, like our bodies or relationships. Thus, we become the successful professionals who have no personal lives or the great moms who are significantly overweight. Although simple in theory, balance is hard in our day-to-day lives.

Dr. White: "Whenever I think about balance, I remember sitting with my own training therapist during graduate school. At some point, he stopped and asked me, 'Kristen, what do they call the person who graduates first in your class?' Easy, I thought—the valedictorian. 'Good. And what do they call the person who graduates last?' Hmm…not so easy. I was stumped, in fact. The answer? 'Doctor.' That's right, the person who graduates last in a doctoral program is still called a doctor. Now, clearly, this story was not told for me to justify laziness. Laziness was never my problem though. Myopic focus was my problem. The point of the story was to teach me that I could be successful academically and professionally without this being the entirety of my life. I didn't have to get 100% on every test or an A+ on every paper; in fact, this probably wasn't a very good idea if it meant that I was exhausted and completely out of balance. I actually learned more by allowing myself to rest, invest in relationships, exercise, and otherwise be healthy in a balanced way…even if it meant getting a few B's."

Sometimes, B's do mean balance. While balance is simple in theory, in actual practice it may require us to adjust the way we pursue our goals, such as moving slower or accepting some imperfection. This doesn't mean we can't achieve excellence or otherwise meet our goals. It just means the path to our goals may look a little different or take a little longer than we originally thought.

In spite of this cost, balance is worth it for two reasons: First, we are better able to enjoy the process; second, we end up with greater holistic success in the end. We'll talk more about this in later chapters. For now, note that holistic integration of the five key areas of our lives—mind, body, heart, relationships, and work—requires us to live in a balanced way.

Putting It into Practice

Before we dive into our first attempt to apply and practice this material, let's review: We are whole, integrated people. In order to achieve true success and happiness, we have to attend to, and seek wellness in, all of the important areas of us and our lives. The five key areas for us to consider are our minds, bodies, hearts, relationships, and work. While it often seems easier to myopically focus on only one of these areas, balancing them tends to lead to greater happiness and success in both the short- and long-term.

This is what it means to take in the whole picture. As with Van Gogh's painting, "Starry Night," it's not enough to simply attend to the details. To focus on only one or two details will probably cause us to miss what's really important. In order to really understand and flourish in life, we have to look at the whole picture. Yes, this means noticing the details—but without making the picture about any one of them alone. Like Van Gogh, life is about putting the details together to make something beautiful that far transcends any of the details by themselves.

Ready to begin making something truly beautiful? Take a few minutes to thoughtfully rate yourself in the following areas and then respond to the questions for reflection. Please note that some of these questions may be difficult to answer for a few reasons. First, they're subjective. "Happiness," for example, might mean something slightly different to each one of us. That's okay. It's important to simply take enough time to ensure the results are accurate and meaningful to us individually. On that note, it may also be hard to answer some of these questions because it's hard to admit we struggle in some of these areas. Keep in mind that no one else will see the answers, so this is a safe place to be honest. Ready? Then dive in!

	Extremely unhealthy and/or unsatisfied	*Moderately unhealthy and/or unsatisfied*	*Somewhat unhealthy and/or unsatisfied*	*Somewhat healthy and/or satisfied*	*Moderately healthy and/or satisfied*	*Extremely healthy and/or satisfied*
Body	1	2	3	4	5	6
Mind	1	2	3	4	5	6
Heart	1	2	3	4	5	6
Work & finances	1	2	3	4	5	6
Relationships	1	2	3	4	5	6
Sense of balance	1	2	3	4	5	6
Overall happiness	1	2	3	4	5	6
Overall success	1	2	3	4	5	6

Questions for Reflection

1) Are there any surprises as I reflect on the worksheet above?

2) What are the one or two of my strongest areas? What makes them so strong?

3) What are the one or two of my weakest areas? What makes them so weak?

4) On a scale of 1-10, what does this information show me about how good I am, right now, at "taking in the whole picture," or thinking holistically?

5) What motivation, if any, do I have to try to approach life more holistically?

Note: If you find yourself wanting to make some changes in your life or simply live more holistically, great! We have the rest of this book to help you do exactly that, so don't feel like you need to have all the answers now. You're already beginning the journey by looking at the whole picture, and we're just getting started!

Tip #2: Gaze Into the Looking Glass

"Looking glasses" are likely to bring to mind all kinds of images and stories. We may think of Snow White's wicked step-mother gazing into the glass and asking, "Mirror, mirror, on the wall, who's the fairest of them all?" Or perhaps Alice comes to mind as she returns to Wonderland through the mirror above her own fireplace. Interestingly, both of these stories involve looking glasses, or mirrors, that reflect something other than the user's image. Like Harry Potter's magical two-way mirror, these looking glasses show a world beyond our immediate, surface-level surroundings.

What if our mirrors could also show us something deeper and truer than simply a 2-D image of our faces and surroundings? We believe they can. And, no, we're not talking about some magical, mystical objects that show us another world. We're talking about gazing into the looking glass of our souls. We're talking about looking deeply into ourselves. Like the wicked queen, we might not always be happy with what we see there. But like Alice, we're likely to find a fascinating adventure. And, like Harry, this piece of the adventure just might help us move ahead on our journeys or even save our lives along the way.

The truth is that gazing into the looking glass of our souls reveals a nearly bottomless source of information and adventure. But how do we tap this resource? We start by becoming more mindful—mindful of the present moment as well as how we live on a daily basis. We open our eyes and ears to what is within and around us, becoming aware instead of oblivious. We also acknowledge any habits we have that hinder our awareness on a daily basis. All of these steps allow us to gaze into the looking glass of our souls, thus increasing our awareness; connecting us to new sources of information; and leading us into grand, new adventures.

What Is Awareness?

Awareness refers to our ability to be present NOW. It cues us into what's happening both around us and inside of us. We may discover physical sensations, emotions, or thoughts inside of us. We may also discover new sights, smells, sounds, or tastes around us. Awareness is basically a mindfulness of noticing the present moment. Truly, awareness is being present in whatever is happening right now.

> *Dr. Puff:* "Awareness is probably my favorite word. Why? Because I've found awareness to be an unbelievably powerful force in both my life and the life of my clients. One of the biggest moments of awareness in my life was during my graduate program when I finally stopped long enough at Princeton to enjoy the beauty of the park around me. This moment was huge for me because I realized that I had been achieving but not really living. It opened my eyes and allowed me to start shifting the way I lived to something much more satisfying and healthy. Similarly, I've seen the power of awareness over and over in my clients' lives. Sometimes they'd prefer

> that I give them advice or otherwise help them 'fix' things; however, the truth is that we can't change anything until we are really aware of it. Over time, I've discovered that awareness truly helps us to understand ourselves too; it comes with a sense of self-discovery, answering the question, 'Who am I?' in new and deeper ways all the time. Perhaps that's why awareness is my favorite word…and one of the biggest tools I use in life—to help myself and others."

To provide some perspective, let's examine the opposite of awareness: Unconscious living. Remember the last time you arrived home without any sense of how you got there? We've all experienced it, and it's mindlessness, or unconscious living. Awareness on our drive home would involve noticing the freeway; the cars around us; the songs on the radio; and even our own mental, emotional, and physical state. In contrast, unconscious living rushes through life, missing both our surroundings and ourselves.

While we may not always be able to attend to everything in every moment, holistic success requires a certain level of awareness. We must be able to hear our thoughts, notice our feelings, and take in our circumstances. This type of awareness allows us to actually experience and enjoy life as it happens. It also gives us direction regarding what we may want or need in a given moment—just like noticing our sensations of hunger or thirst direct us to eat or drink. Not noticing these physical sensations might lead us to starvation; similarly, not noticing our thoughts, feelings, and circumstances may lead us to significant distress over time. Overall, we need awareness to both experience our lives and be directed in them.

The Appeal of Self-Medicating

Sometimes, it's hard to be aware. It can be hard because we are so busy that we simply forget or run out of time to attend to ourselves and our surroundings. It can also be hard because of what we discover when we are aware. We may really hate our jobs and thus not enjoy the process of noticing what's happening around us when we're at work. Alternatively, perhaps we feel a lot of anxiety or dissatisfaction, and it's difficult for us to feel these things. There are many times and ways that awareness can be difficult or even painful.

Because awareness is sometimes uncomfortable or even painful, we often find ways to avoid it. We call this "self-medicating." Self-medicating refers to our attempts to avoid and/or numb our feelings through unrelated stimuli. Self-medicating may involve rather benign activities like over-eating, numbing out in front of the TV for hours at a time, excessive involvement with video games or social media, or constant shopping. It may also involve things like pornography (or other forms of illicit sexual activity), alcohol, or drugs. Sometimes even using prescribed anti-depressants or their herbal alternatives can be a form of self-medicating as we use them to avoid feeling and facing things.[1] There are many, many ways we self-medicate to avoid our uncomfortable or painful feelings.

The good news and bad news is that self-medicating works. It usually does mask our feelings, allowing us to avoid and forget about our troubles for awhile. It also allows us to continue functioning and maybe even succeeding in some areas of our lives. In fact, sometimes self-medicating our pain is so effective that we don't even consciously realize we're doing it. Whether or not we're aware of our attempts to self-medicate, the times when it is necessary are the exception rather than the rule. For most of us, "medication" of any kind—whether it be Prozac or five hours of TV every night—is generally a short-term solution to a long-term problem.

The problem with using self-medicating as a long-term solution is twofold. First, self-medicating doesn't really solve our problems, so nothing changes or gets better. Actually, because we're ignoring our problems, they are likely to get worse over time. It's kind of like ignoring a cut that then becomes infected and worsens. In this sense, the pain we are feeling is a gift that tells us something is wrong and needs attention. The cost of

---

[1] Please note that we are not against the use of "supplements"—whether they be natural remedies or psychotropic medications. There are many instances when they are necessary and life-saving, as in the cases of severe depression. There are other times where they are at least part of the solution to a long-term issue, such as in the case of bipolar or schizophrenia. Our point is simply that many people use medications as substitute for true emotional healing and freedom, which is what we refer to here.

ignoring this "gift" through self-medication is an ever-worsening problem that may eventually cause us (or some specific area of our lives) to crash and burn.

The second problem with self-medicating is that the behaviors we use to avoid our discomfort or pain usually come with a cost. Eventually, the fact that we are relying on and over-using things to make us feel better adds up: The food causes us to gain weight, the shopping runs up our credit cards, the alcohol becomes an addiction, the drugs result in occupational or legal problems, the sexual issues screw up our relationships, etc., etc. Yes, self-medicating works for a time, but it eventually costs us in multiple ways—sometimes dearly.

The Truth Shall Set Us Free

As hard as it may be to talk about things like painful feelings or our attempts to avoid them through self-medicating, we are doing it for a reason. Here it is: There is more, and there is a better way to get there. We don't have to simply survive life through the use of food, TV, alcohol, shopping, or any other forms of self-medicating. We can actually experience holistic success and happiness on a day-to-day basis.

In order to experience this success and happiness, we have to begin with awareness. We have to know what is really happening in and around us. Without this awareness, we are like puppets on strings. We react to circumstances and events in our lives automatically and sometimes even impulsively, without even consciously knowing what we're doing. It's like the college student who returns home for the holidays. No matter how much that student has changed, he or she often begins responding to family members reflexively—out of old habits and scripts. This student isn't consciously making any choices; instead, like a puppet on a string, other people's choices and the circumstances of life are pulling the strings for the student and thus determining how he/she responds.

Unfortunately, living like a puppet on a string is way more common than we'd like to admit. It's a part of life: We develop habits and patterns for everything we do, from how we interact with people to what, when, and how much we eat. These habits aren't always a bad thing; sometimes they help us to respond quickly and even healthily. Many times, however, they need some work. The first step in working on these habits is to become aware of what they are and how they impact us. The first step is realizing where and how we are puppets—tied to strings that someone or something else is pulling.

> *Dr. White:* "During college, I realized that I was a puppet in many ways. I was very intellectually developed, studying philosophy and looking into life's deepest questions. Emotions were another story, however. I was pretty unaware of my emotions and how they impacted me. Over time, I realized that my emotions created certain patterns of behaving that I engaged in unconsciously. For example, when I felt sad, I tended to withdraw and eat. I was completely unaware of this pattern at the time—simply engaging it reflexively, like a puppet.

> As I became aware of it, however, I began to have options. Suddenly I could choose how I responded to my sadness. I discovered many options that were better than numbing out through food or withdrawal—such as calling a friend, journaling, or going for a walk. It took time to make these better options into habits. The first step on this journey toward freedom, however, was awareness."

As we've acknowledged, it can be uncomfortable to increase our awareness of ourselves and how we're living. It may not feel good to realize just how many places we are puppets, reflexively responding to the environment without any conscious thought at all. In reality, though, this awareness is the first step in cutting the strings and becoming free. Whether we like it or not, there is no way around—we must go through. It is only as we become aware of ourselves, our circumstances, and how we normally respond to life that we can begin to make real changes that lead to holistic success, happiness, and freedom.

Putting It Into Practice

Awareness is a powerful tool. It's simple in theory: Just being attentive to whatever is happening now—in our bodies, minds, hearts, surroundings, etc. In practice, however, it's often much harder. It's harder because we get busy and because sometimes what we discover when we are aware is uncomfortable or painful. It can be tempting at such times to self-medicate, or numb out using unrelated stimuli—like food, shopping, alcohol, or sex. Unfortunately, while self-medicating works for the moment, it usually comes with long-term costs that make it a problem. While awareness might be the harder way sometimes, the alternative is living as a puppet, unconsciously controlled by the things around us. In contrast, awareness opens the door for us to see (and eventually cut) the strings, leading to real success, happiness, and freedom.

The truth is that awareness allows us to gaze into the magical, mystical looking glass of our souls. We get to see past the surface-level image of our face and surroundings, into the depth of ourselves and our lives. And what an adventure that can be! Almost all of the chapters in this book will help you embark on this adventure in new ways. For example, we'll look deeply into our thoughts, noticing not only the content but also the themes, valence (i.e., positive or negative), and intensity. We'll also look into our emotions, examining how we currently engage with (or avoid) them and how a healthy awareness of them can add color and vibrancy to our lives. There are many ways and many areas in which we can gaze into the looking glass of ourselves, transforming our obliviousness into awareness.

To start this process, we'd like to propose a challenge: Spend at least 20 minutes in a quiet place with nothing other than yourself. Ideally, this challenge will be done outside. Wherever it is completed, the place must be free of distractions. And, yes, "free of distractions" means no cell phones, computers, ipods, books, food, or other distractions. Literally, it is 20 minutes (or more) with nothing but yourself. It is okay to walk during this time, although sitting may be preferable because it helps many people focus more completely on their surroundings. Any posture is really fine, however, except for laying down (since this will likely lead to sleeping). In summary, the challenge is a minimum of 20 minutes alone, sitting or standing, in a quiet place.

During this time, it's important to simply notice your surroundings and see what comes up inside of you. To begin, take a look around. What do you see? Are there smells and sounds you can pick out? Can you feel or even taste anything around you? Take some time to simply notice these sensations. Try not to judge them. Simply take them in. Simultaneously, take some time to notice what's happening inside of you. Are there any noticeable physical sensations in your body, such as tightness in your back or chest, butterflies in your stomach, or heaviness in your eyelids? Also, what kind of thoughts and feelings run through your body and mind? Again, try not to judge these thoughts, feelings, or sensations. Just notice and be aware—both inside and out.

This challenge may be easy or very difficult. It will probably be easier for people who are used to having time with quiet and stillness. In contrast, for those who typically run through life at a mile a minute, the challenge will likely be more difficult. In addition, the "space" it creates may be peaceful or it may be very anxiety-provoking. For some people, it may create a sense of well-being or even gratitude. For others, the space may give way to exhaustion. Many people may find that their minds continue to race at such a pace that even this "space" doesn't feel quiet. For those who have more difficulty, it may be helpful to focus on one's breathing, feeling it go slowly in and out as a way to ground oneself. The bottom-line, however, is simply to let our experiences be what they are—with awareness but not judgment. Then, after completing the challenge, take some time to reflect on the following questions.

Questions for Reflection

1) What was my overall experience of this challenge? Did it feel long or short, good or bad?

2) What did I notice in my surroundings and myself? Was there anything I became more aware of?

3) Did I find myself craving anything during this time, like food, activity, people, or even sex?

4) If I did notice particular cravings, is it possible I use my craved object to keep myself from awareness and even self-medicate at times? If so, what feeling, thought, or experience are these cravings covering?

5) What does this experience tell me about my overall level of awareness on a moment-to-moment basis in my life?

Tip #3: Be a Visionary

There are many types (and definitions) of visionaries. Some visionaries, such as those who have incorrectly predicted the end of the world, have unrealistic ideas of the present or future. Other visionaries have idealistic ideas that may be idyllic but are theoretically possible and perhaps even genius. Depending on one's political views, the Founding Fathers of America may be considered this second type of visionary. A third kind of visionary consists of those who have religious visions of some sort, such as Joseph Smith and Mohammad. Truly, visionaries run the gamut and exist on a spectrum from impractical and out-of-touch to geniuses with great foresight.

Here, we refer to the type of visionaries who have great foresight and imagination. These are not people who miss reality or escape it. Instead, these are the people who have enough foresight to see trends, imagine the future impact, and make necessary changes to achieve the best possible outcome. These are the people who are looking past their immediate circumstances to plan ahead—imagining and then creating the best possible circumstances for themselves and others. Many consider Steve Jobs to be an example of a visionary in business. In reality, these visionaries with great foresight and imagination exist in all arenas of life.

Imagine what life would be like if we could encounter these visionaries in our day-to-day lives. Better yet, what if we could *be* these visionaries? What if we could clearly see trends and envision the future for ourselves, using this information to achieve the best outcome today as well as in 10, 20, or even 50 years? In a lot of ways, we actually can be these visionaries. We have enough information—both anecdotal and researched—to know quite a bit about how our decisions today will impact our futures in the short and long-term. For the greatest holistic success, we must use this information to envision our future and make wise, long-term decisions.

Thinking Long-Term

So what does it mean to envision the future and think long-term? It means that we consider the consequences of our choices, particularly the long-term consequences. We think about how our food intake will impact our body in 20 minutes and 20 years. We consider what the consequences will be on our credit—both now and in 5 years—if we buy that new car today. We even notice what impact our hobbies have on our hearts and bodies—both today and well into the future. Thinking long-term really just means that we are mindful of the consequences of our actions.

We must utilize a lot of different kids of data to fully consider the consequences of our choices. For example, we know from both research and anecdotes of our friends that we will probably fare better over time if we eat more salads than hamburgers. In contrast, we may need to tap into our personal financial picture as well as general information regarding purchases to determine whether now is a good time to buy that new car. And, coming in on the opposite end of the spectrum, we may have to be mindful of our actual experience of doing yoga versus having coffee with our friends as we determine the best hobby to enjoy today. Considering the consequences of our actions involves taking into account all kinds of data, ranging from experiential to intellectual as well as anecdotal to researched.

This book is all about packaging the best anecdotal and researched information into practical tips so that we can find greater holistic success—both today and in 50 years. We'll talk about a lot of the details as we move forward. For now, we want to emphasize that we must consider all sources of data available to us in order to make the best decisions today. Ideally, these decisions consider the impact of our actions both today and in the long-term. The truth is that while we might experience pleasure in the short-term if we only focus on today, our futures will be much better if we live with tomorrow in view.

Accumulating Impacts

Thinking long-term is important because our choices catch up with us over time. The areas that we invest and make wise decisions in now pay off in the long-run, and areas that we make poor decisions in now eventually cost us. This happens because our choices accumulate over time. Simply imagine those Hershey kisses we grab off our co-workers desk a couple of times a day. Four or five small pieces of chocolate a day don't make a big difference, right? Wrong. Over the course of a year, those candies are likely to accumulate in a weight gain of seven or eight pounds![2] Whether we're talking about food or other areas of our lives, the impact of our choices may be subtle at first, but they do eventually catch up to us.

> *Dr. Puff:* "This truth has always been particularly clear for me in the contrast between my two grandmothers. While both lived into their 90's, one was a thinker and one was a doer. The thinker liked to sit, learn, and ruminate on ideas throughout her life. This served her mind well, in that she was cognitively healthy until the end of her life; however, it did not serve her body, as she had a number of physical problems for years. In contrast, the 'doer' grandmother was very physically active throughout her life, but she never spent much time learning, reading, or otherwise engaging her mind. While she remained physically healthy until she passed away, she suffered from Alzheimer's as her mind deteriorated. These two grandmothers have always been an example to me of the old saying, 'We reap what we sow.'"

Whether we like it or not, it's true—in the long run, we do reap what we sow. Why? Because the impact of our decisions accumulates over time. Even though we theoretically know this, and we all want to be healthy later in life, we often forget that things will catch up to us

[2] Calculations based on an extra 3,500 calories equating to one pound.

as we make daily decisions. While we sometimes turn a blind eye to the consequences of our actions, more often than not we simply fail to take into account the accumulative impact of our choices. We don't add up the candies we grab "on the run," and we forget that how we use our brains or bodies today matters when we're 90-years-old. But it's true: The consequences of our actions accumulate, and they do matter in the end.

Our Habits Matter

The fact that our choices catch up to us over time doesn't mean that we have to obsess over each and every little decision we make every day. We probably won't die from a heart attack if we drive through fast food for dinner tonight, nor will we ruin our marriages by working late for one week. We all have unusual days and seasons when things are especially busy or stressful, and they sometimes necessitate decisions that are focused on merely getting through today. If these crazy, busy seasons and momentary decisions are the exception to the rule, they really don't need to be a big deal.

What matters is the typical, every day decisions we make and the habits that we form around them. If we start eating fast food every night, we probably are going to start gaining weight and eventually begin to have high cholesterol or other health problems. Similarly, if we work so late every night that we don't have time to connect with our partner or kids, we will eventually be pretty disconnected from them and our relationships will begin to suffer. In this sense, although our momentary decisions may not determine the course of our lives, the habits and routines we get into are likely to have a huge impact on our overall health and success.

Our habits are the things we do every day without thinking. They are the behaviors we've chosen so many times that we now do them without any conscious choice at all. Our habits may involve the hours we work, the ways we interact with our partners or other people in our lives, the foods that we eat, the hobbies we engage in, and so much more. It's these habits that really make the difference over time.

Compare, for example, two women we know: One who is 80-years-old and one is 25. The 80-year-old woman has taken such good care of her health that she was able to enjoy a trip that involved hiking 10 miles per day, while the 25-year-old had to give up running because she had been smoking since high school. It clearly wasn't one cigarette that caused the 25-year-old to give up running, nor was it one work out that led the 80-year-old to be in such good shape that she was able to hike for vacation. What made the difference for both of these people was the habits that they formed.

It's easy to see, then, why it's critical to think long-term in the habits we create. While our momentary decisions may not make or break us, our habits just might. Why? We already know the answer to this: Because our habits are things we do again and again, and the consequences of our actions accumulate over time. Hence, it turns out that it's especially important to think long-term in regards to the habits and routines we create in our lives.

Yes, It Can Be Hard

It's probably important to acknowledge that thinking long-term can sometimes be difficult or even require sacrifice. It can be difficult because it often goes against the grain. We live in a world that's geared toward immediate gratification and comfort, so long-term thinking is not always popular or mainstream. Just think of all the prepared food we eat because it takes too much time or effort to grocery shop and cook. We lead such busy lives that it's often easiest to just make decisions focused on the moment.

Thinking long-term requires us to go against the grain, and, yes, it sometimes also requires sacrifice. Imagine, again, that one's choice is between a quick, fast-food meal or a healthy meal, prepared at home. Choosing the healthy meal takes more time—time that could otherwise be spent elsewhere. It's true, thinking long-term sometimes requires us to make less popular choices that may also require more from us in terms of time or effort.

> *Dr. White:* "A favorite saying of Dr. Puff's is, '*You can have anything you want in life, you just can't have everything.*' I have to admit, the first time I heard this, I bristled more than a little bit. 'What do you mean I can't have it all?!' I wondered. 'Why would I lose out on anything by reaching for health?' After I mulled this over for a few days, I had an epiphany: Dr. Puff's statement is in direct contradiction to the feminist notion that we can have

it all. Although I'm thankful to the feminist movement for the freedom it has brought women in their roles and choices, I am increasingly aware of the pressure it has birthed for women to have and do it all—career, family, etc. While I want all of those things, I'm very aware that I can't really be super-mom, super-career woman, super-wife, and super-friend all at the same time…especially not while actually taking care of myself. This point was driven home to me when my husband and I begun to move toward starting a family. We were both excited to have children, and I was very thankful to have a career that I could still invest in while being home much of the time with my kids. However, I was also aware that my career would slow down once the baby-fun started. I simply wouldn't have as many hours to see clients, write, or do other professional activities. This didn't mean that I couldn't be great in each of these areas of my life, but it would likely take me longer to meet certain goals, like establishing a practice of my own."

The reality is that balance sometimes requires some hard choices and even sacrifice. We can have a lot—more, in fact, than many of us (ourselves included) may have ever dreamed was possible. However, we can't necessarily "have it all" right this very minute. As we said earlier, things may take longer or look a little different than we originally thought. For instance, in addition to slowing down in her career a bit, Dr. White and her husband also had to wait a little longer to buy a home because they were choosing to prioritize time with each other and their (soon-to-be!) children. Wellness in all areas of our lives simply takes more time than wellness in just one area of our lives.

So, yes, we admit it: Thinking long-term is not always easy. In fact, sometimes it's actually difficult. It may require us to go against the grain, making different choices than our friends, family, or simply the culture at large. It may also take more time or effort. This is especially true at first—when we're changing from short- to long-term thinking. Long-term thinking can be a habit that becomes easier with time; however, we acknowledge that compared to just taking the easiest solution in each and every moment, long-term thinking can be difficult.

Debunking the Myth the Healthy Behaviors are Unpleasant

While we admit that thinking about the long-term can sometimes be difficult, we absolutely disagree with the widely-held idea that long-term or "healthy" decisions are unappealing. We live in a society that seems to believe that what's good for us is generally unpleasant. We learn to "work out" because we *should.* We eat salads (or our brussel sprouts or liver) because we're supposed to, really wishing they'd taste like hamburgers. Perhaps we even pry ourselves away from our favorite TV shows to play with our kids or connect with our partner because we know intellectually this is important. We continually try to push ourselves to do what we "should" instead of what we "want."

Dr. Puff: "There seems to be a widespread belief that the things which are 'bad' for us are the most fun; however, I've discovered that what's good for us doesn't have to be icky or painful—it can be quite enjoyable. In fact, this is how I explain my transition from French fries to green, organic juice. Allow me to explain: I grew up in Iowa on meat and potatoes. My idea of eating healthy was to add an extra serving of French fries so that I fit in some 'veggies.' (Yes, I really thought French fries qualified as veggies because they are potatoes.) At the time, if you'd suggested that I drink a green, fruit and vegetable-packed juice for breakfast, I would have thought you were crazy. I might have even gagged at the taste of it. However, after slowly learning about nutrition over the years and making the transition to healthier foods, I now love my green, morning juice. A lot of people look at it and think they'd prefer to keep their French fries, but I honestly don't enjoy those anymore. I truly prefer and delight in the flavors of my juice."

How can this be? Don't French fries always taste better than green juice? Not necessarily. In actuality, our bodies biologically adjust to the foods we are eating. Our taste buds die and are renewed approximately every three weeks. Plus, our brains create new receptors for the types of foods we are eating (e.g., salty, sweet).[i] In other words, we crave meat, carbs, and sugar because we are acclimated to eating them. If we switched what we were eating, we'd adjust fairly quickly and enjoy it just as much. Actually, we'll talk about this more when we get to talking about the body, but we contend that we actually enjoy the good stuff more because it gives us great energy, digestion, etc.—in addition to tasting just as good.

Whether or not you concede that last idea yet, the point is this: We can enjoy the things that are good for us *today*. It sometimes takes a little time to adjust, but our bodies eventually begin to prefer the good stuff. Just think about the fact that Dr. Puff now enjoys green, power juice while experiencing French fries as pretty disgusting. Although we have acknowledged these type of long-term decisions can be difficult at first, they do not really need to cost us any of the pleasure or joy in life. In fact, we'll show you throughout this book how we can actually experience more happiness, pleasure, and joy today when we make healthy decisions for tomorrow.

Putting It into Practice

Overall, the important point to understand is that we must think about the long-term consequences of our actions in order to experience holistic success in our lives. This is one of the ways we can take in the whole picture and be balanced—by using all of the data at our disposal to consider the long-term impact of our choices. This doesn't mean that we have to scrutinize every little decision we ever make, but we do need to pay close attention to our habits because the effects of those behaviors accumulate over time. Sometimes it is hard to make wise choices in our habits, but the payoff makes it worth it—both today and in the future. Clearly, it's time we begin finding things that feel good now *and* benefit us in the long-term.

This is what is means to be a visionary in our own lives: Having foresight regarding how the decisions we make today will affect tomorrow. It's imaging the future impact of our choices and making necessary changes to achieve the best possible outcome—today as well as in 10, 20, or even 50 years. We'll share specific wisdom, research, and tips throughout this book that will help us figure out the paths to the best outcomes in specific areas of our lives. For now though, it's important that we reflect on the paths we're already taking.

Ready to be a visionary in your own life? Start by completing the chart on the next page. Simply fill in your activities for a typical week. Be as specific as possible, including, for example, the foods you eat and specific leisure activities you pursue rather than simply stating "eat" or "rest." Clearly, your schedule and activities may vary from week to week; consequently, it's important to just make statements about your most typical or routine behavior. When you've finished the chart, take a few minutes to answer the reflection questions below. These questions will help you assess the long-term impact of your current habits and activities—setting you firmly on the path of being a visionary in your own life.

	Sunday	Monday	Tuesday	Wednesday	Thursday	Friday	Saturday
6:00am							
7:00am							
8:00am							
9:00am							
10:00am							
11:00am							
12:00pm							
1:00pm							
2:00pm							
3:00pm							
4:00pm							
5:00pm							
6:00pm							
7:00pm							
8:00pm							
9:00pm							
10:00pm							
11:00pm							
12:00am							
1:00am							
2:00am							
3:00am							
4:00am							
5:00am							

Questions for Reflection

1) Is there anything I notice about my current habits by completing the chart above?

2) If my current habits were to stay the same for the next *2 years*, how would this impact:

a) my body?

b) my mind?

c) my heart?

d) my work/finances?

e) my relationships?

3) If my current habits were to stay the same for the next *40 years*, how would this impact:

a) my body?

b) my mind?

c) my heart?

d) my work/finances?

e) my relationships?

4) As I envision my potential future, are there changes I'm aware of needing for greater long-term effects?

5) Is there one specific area that I'd like to focus on first?

Tying It All Together

Like it or not, we are holistic beings. In order to achieve true success and happiness, we must seek wellness in all of the important areas of our lives, including our minds, bodies, hearts, relationships, and work. While it may be easier for us to myopically focus on only one or two of these areas, balancing them tends to lead to greater happiness and success in both the short- and long-term. This is what it means to *take in the whole picture*—noticing all the critical details, while putting them together to make something beautiful that far transcends any of the details by themselves.

Where do we start in noticing and putting together the details for a holistically healthy life? We begin with awareness. Awareness involves being attentive to whatever is happening now—in our bodies, minds, hearts, surroundings, etc. Sometimes the things we discover with our awareness are wonderful, and sometimes they are uncomfortable or painful. In the latter times, it can be tempting to self-medicate, or numb out using unrelated stimuli—like food, shopping, alcohol, or sex. Unfortunately, living this way usually comes with long-term problems…not to mention that it reduces us to living like a puppet, unconsciously controlled by the strings around us. In contrast, awareness allows us to *gaze into the looking glass* of our souls, helping us to see past the surface-level image of our face and surroundings and move toward real health.

As we attempt to move toward health, one of the things we need to be particularly attentive to is the long-term consequences of our actions. This is another way we can move toward holistically healthy lives—by using all of the data at our disposal to consider the long-term impact of our choices. This doesn't mean that we have to scrutinize every little decision we ever make, but we do need to pay close attention to our habits because the effects of those behaviors accumulate over time. This is what it means to *be a visionary* in our own lives: Having foresight regarding how the decisions we make today will affect tomorrow.

As we take these steps—adopting a holistic view, increasing our awareness, and thinking long-term—we are setting up the foundation for holistically healthy living. We are like the dancer who wisely attends to everything from his steps to his partner to the music. We are rejecting the ridiculously common notion of finding success through utter imbalance, choosing instead to recognize that we are holistic beings. Each area of us and our lives matters. And we will work on developing each and every one. Ready? We've discussed the big picture; next, we'll start breaking down the key areas.

Part II: Mind

In addition to emphasizing a holistic, balanced stance, a great dancer also knows about the importance of focus. Young children know this intuitively, throwing out their arms and twirling with no cares or distractions in the world. Professional, adult ballerinas often have to re-learn the abandon that comes with this type of focus. After all, they could have all the skill, muscles, and talent in the world, but they'd be unable to employ it effectively without focus. Somehow, for a really stellar performance, the professional dancer must be able to take all of her training and talent, and, like the child, channel it fully into the present moment. Even for a professional dancer who's all about demonstrating her skill with the body, what's happening in her mind matters.

Similarly for us, what's happening in our minds is critical. The mind, again, can be conceived of as the source of our thoughts. Comparing our thoughts to transportation may help us to understand them. Our thoughts may be about a variety of topics, just as there are a variety of cars on the road. There are also both "good" and "bad" neighborhoods to drive these cars in, just as our minds have "good" and "bad" attitudes and perspectives. Lastly, our thoughts may also be more or less active or still, similar to how we may travel on free-flowing freeways or in dead-stopped traffic. These three aspects of the mind—the type of thoughts, valence (positive or negative), and activity level—all matter.

Unfortunately, most of us don't give much thought to our minds. Sometimes, we may not even be aware of what's happening there, and we certainly don't think we have much control over it. We often act as if our cars, neighborhoods, and traffic patterns are dictated and set. We may realize the clunker we drive is getting us into trouble as it causes us to break down throughout life, such as on Anxiety Avenue. Or perhaps the traffic we run into wastes lots of time, derailing us from what we really want to be doing, like spending time at Family Park instead of Work City. In spite of these common habits of the mind, we don't usually stop to attend to and change them.

The amazing news today is this: We actually have a ton of control over all aspects of the mind. We can change from a clunker in a sketchy neighborhood to a luxury car in an upscale one, as we move from negative thoughts about things that don't work to positive thoughts about what we can control and where we feel blessed. We can also rework our minds to avoid much of the heavy traffic, finding a place of stillness and peace as our minds slow down and focus on the present. Yes, we can control many aspects of the mind.

Like the spontaneous child and expert dancer we aspire to be, we must control our minds so that they don't sabotage our dance through life. We want our minds to provide us the mental clarity and focus of the best dancers. This focus allows us to believe the best and enjoy the performance at the given moment. As a result, this section will talk about the various aspects of the mind, defining each and teaching us to take control of our minds, moving from the negative busyness that often consumes us internally to a positive calmness that can pervade our life and dance.

Tip #4: Quiet the Critic

Think, for a minute, about watching a sports match. Whether it's football, hockey, or even table tennis, there is one common element. Any guesses? Yes, the competition is there. But we're talking about something more subtle and interesting: The commentator. That's right, no matter the sport, there is a commentator who breaks down every moment and play, telling you what is happening and assessing whether it is good or bad.

These sports commentators can range from helpful to annoying. If we're still learning the sport, watching it from afar, or want a second opinion, hearing their running dialogue can be helpful. Let's be honest though—at times, the commentary can get pretty old and even annoying. In some moments, we've even put the TV on mute to enjoy the game without the commentator's running dialogue. Yep, these sports commentators are helpful, but they can get to be too much.

Similarly, our minds tend to have a running dialogue that can range from helpful to downright annoying. Our brains are built to assess everything—telling us what is safe and dangerous, good and bad, etc.—to help us survive. At its core, this is a fantastically helpful system which helps us to quickly assess and respond to our environment. Unfortunately, for many of us, this systems seems to have run amuck. It's gone from simple messages about what's safe to an elaborate dialogue on how our hair looks today, what we ate for lunch, what the person next to us is thinking, how much we accomplished today, and even what might happen next year. Our minds have become detailed commentators and even critics—constantly noticing, assessing, judging, and (far too often) criticizing everything that happens in our lives, both internally and externally.

We call this running commentary "self-talk." Self-talk involves all of the things we say to ourselves about our lives, our actions, and even our thoughts. We'll talk more about what self-talk is in a minute. For now, it's important to notice that this type of commentary is usually running in our minds. It can sometimes be somewhat subconscious, so that we don't really notice it's happening. Even when we do notice, it sometimes feels so engrained that we simply think this is the way things are for everyone. The truth, however, is that we don't need (or want) to live with an overwhelming commentary running constantly in our minds. Why? Because this internal commentary, or "self-talk," impacts us whether or not we are aware of it. In this chapter, we'll talk more about what self-talk is, where it comes from, and how it impacts us. Later, we'll talk about how to quiet it too, especially if it's a critical commentary.

Two Kinds of Self-Talk

Self-talk, again, is the internal commentary that happens in our minds. It's the thoughts we have about ourselves, our actions, and more. Like the sports castors, most of our commentary tends to be pretty incessant. Usually, it involves a detailed description of what is happening and an assessment of the "players'" talents (i.e., ourselves and the people we interact with). The running dialogue, or commentary, may also involve things like how past "stats" (i.e., events) come into play or where the players may go in the future based on the results of this "game." In other words, we have a running internal dialogue about us, others, and circumstances—past, present, and even future. The dialogue of both sports commentators and our minds is actually quite multi-faceted, including everything from noticing to judging as well as past-ruminating to future-forecasting.

In the midst of all this diversity, there are always two kinds of self-talk running through our heads: Internal and external. Internal self-talk encompasses thoughts we have about ourselves. These thoughts include commentary on who we are, the choices we make, and even other thoughts or impulses we have. For example, imagine getting dressed in the morning. Many people have an internal commentary related to what clothes they choose, how those clothes look on them, how long it's taking to get ready, etc. This commentary may simply *notice* our clothes, hair, timing, and other details, or it may *critique* different aspects. Critiquing may involve negative thoughts about how our hair or clothes look today, how long we are taking to get ready, the fact that we forgot to do laundry yesterday, or any other imaginable thing related to what we are experiencing. Both the thoughts that notice and those that assess or critique our appearance and behavior are considered internal self-talk.

Similarly, external self-talk notices and assesses things outside of ourselves. Like all self-talk, this commentary occurs in our minds, even though it's about things outside of ourselves. For example, we may notice and assess other people's behavior or even their intentions. Simply imagine being cut off on the freeway. It's quite common to think that the person was being rude, is a poor driver, or possibly even considers him/herself more important than others. These thoughts are all commentary about who that person is, what they intend, and how they behave. Similarly, we may have thoughts about the world—whether it is a fair, safe, and trustworthy place or not. Either way, external self-talk is an internal dialogue or commentary about the world around us.

Dr. White: "I returned this week from a very full, out-of-town, four-day conference. Like most of us when we return from being out-of-town, I was behind on both work and personal tasks (e.g., laundry, groceries) as a result of being at the conference. Nonetheless, I took the morning to relax and reflect on what I learned and then dove into all that was waiting on my task list. I felt engaged and positive about all that I was working on and getting done…until my husband came home and asked how my day was. I suddenly felt like I couldn't figure out exactly how all of these miscellaneous tasks had taken up my entire day. And then the commentary was really off and running! All of a sudden, I was thinking about how much I had to do, assessing whether I had really worked hard enough during the day, trying to figure out when I would get it all done (and what would happen if I didn't), etc., etc. This was an exhausting reminder to me of how quickly this running commentary, or self-talk, can creep in and take over our minds."

It may be increasingly clear that self-talk is simply the stories we tell ourselves. These stories may be about us or others. They may be benign—as when Dr. White noticed she had a lot to do, or they may be critical—such as when Dr. White began assessing her work and feeling she had not gotten enough done. These stories may also be quite simple or very elaborate. The more elaborate ones often tell us long, involved stories about why we think something happened or what we think will happen next (e.g., Dr. White postulating what would happen if she didn't get all of her work done). Either way, these stories tend to *feel like facts* as they regularly and consistently run through our heads, commentating about both internal and external aspects of life.

Where Did it Start?

The commentary of self-talk originates in our early years. At a very young age, we begin to notice what we do and do not like. We notice that cookies taste good, and perhaps brushing our teeth does not. We like playing with our toys, and we do not like sharing them or having them taken away. This is a natural process of figuring out our desires, opinions, and even voice. It's also natural that these desires and opinions get internalized as self-talk—a voice which continues to commentate in our minds on whether things we receive and do are "good" or "bad."

So how does this self-talk get turned around to commentate on our own behavior, thoughts, and feelings? A lot of this comes from other people. We take the voices of mom, dad, teachers, or other significant adults (and, much later, peers and partners) and make them our own. For example, if we had a primary caregiver who was very critical of us, constantly telling us what we did was bad or wrong, we are likely to begin treating ourselves this way. We may or may not verbalize these opinions about ourselves and our behavior, but we are likely to run them through our minds either way. On the flip side, if we had a caregiver who was positive and loving, we may internalize and replay thoughts of love, acceptance, and grace toward ourselves. Whatever messages others gave us tend to get internalized into our own self-talk.

Self-talk, then, simply comes from the process of interacting with our environment. We take in the voices of others, and we develop our own voice as we learn to form opinions and commentate on the world. As we do this, we tend to develop themes and patterns of self-talk that replay again and again. For instance, our self-talk may be focused on our physical appearance (e.g., "I'm looking fat today"), fun (e.g., "As soon as I get this work done, I'll enjoy…"), success (e.g., "When I finish this job, I'll get that promotion"), or even something like sex (no illustration needed!). In addition to these themes, we may also have patterns of self-talk, such as criticism (e.g., "That was so stupid!") or planning (e.g., "Right when I get up tomorrow morning, I'll begin by…and then I'll…"). We may also have self-talk that is either focused on the past (e.g., "I still can't believe my husband made that comment about my hair last year") or the future (e.g., "I'll slow down as soon as I finish school"). Although these are just a few examples, our themes and patterns of self-talk tend to get reinforced as we replay them again and again in our minds.

In addition to being reinforced by simple repetition, our themes and patterns of self-talk often seem to be reinforced by our experiences as well. We say "seem to be" because this phenomenon is not quite as straightforward as it appears. Allow us a moment to explain. It's impossible for us to attend to every single thing that's happening or every diverse aspect of our experience. As a result, our brains are constantly sorting through huge amounts of information, trying to pick the most salient pieces and interpret them as accurately as possible. As our brains go through this process over and over, they develop a sort of shorthand that biases us toward making similar assessments to those that fit before. Consequently, we sometimes feel that new experiences reinforce old ones; as it turns out, our brains gravitate toward noticing the pieces that support the same old conclusions and dismissing the pieces that don't. In other words, we are more likely to notice experiences (and interpret events in such a way) that already fit our self-talk rather than create new messages in our brains.

Hence, self-talk is really developing throughout our lives. It starts in our young childhood as we develop opinions and a voice about the world. It also gets shaped during our interactions with other significant people, such as early caregivers. From these two sources, we often develop themes and patterns of thought directed at ourselves or others. We then continue to reinforce these themes and patterns in two ways: (1) Our habitual repetition or rehashing of them, and (2) The fact that we notice aspects of our experience that support our current self-talk rather than contradict it. Hence, our self-talk is an engrained, yet dynamic, pattern of thinking and being that develops throughout our lives.

The Good, the Bad, and the In-Between

So what do we make of this mental phenomenon called self-talk? The truth is that it has pluses and minuses. On the positive side, self-talk represents our brains' mental shorthand. The process of commentating on everything is part of our internal process of assessing our lives and our environment. This quick assessment is actually important; if we really had to stop and deliberate on every new situation or piece of the environment as if we were seeing it for the first time, we'd never get anywhere. In addition to taking forever, this would leave us more vulnerable to dangerous situations because our response time would be so slow. In the sense that self-talk represents our brains' quick process of assessing, it's definitely a plus.

Unfortunately, this quick process of assessing is quite sloppy. Just imagine a computer that only assessed part of the variables to any equation—it would definitely make a lot of mistakes! Our brains do this too. They are assessing so quickly that they often misinterpret aspects of our lives. Dr. White's story was a great example of this. She's accustomed to working on one or two larger projects for every "work at home" day. On the Monday she returned from her conference, all of the miscellaneous projects precluded any of this time, so her brain quickly made the (mistaken) assessment that she had wasted time and not gotten enough done. Clearly, when we (or our brains) do things hastily, we are bound to make more mistakes.

In addition to making sloppy mistakes, self-talk is also a problem because it's loud and verbose. Of course, the volume and quantity of our self-talk can vary considerably; however, when left to themselves, our brains tend to turn up both the volume and quantity. This means that we may be telling ourselves such loud, elaborate stories that we are missing out on our lives as they happen. Simply imagine if Dr. White had continued down the path her brain was taking her. The rest of her night would have been spent feeling bad and worrying about her workload; even if she was with her husband or friends physically, her mind would have kept her from really being present and engaging in the time. This is the second problem with self-talk: It tends to be too loud and too talkative—to the point that it can overrun the actual moment we're experiencing.

Dr. Puff: "I was struck by the power (and potential negative consequences) of self-talk just this week. I was out hiking with my 13-year-old yellow lab,

Einstein. As we were climbing a hill, Einstein's legs collapsed under him and he fell down. I immediately walked over, helped him up, and continued along the path. Einstein kept going and was quickly back to exploring his surroundings. Together, we finished enjoying our walk. Later in the day, I thought more about this incident. It struck me how many people would have begun worrying and telling themselves that their dog must be getting old, his hips are deteriorating, and he may not last much longer. The stories I could have told myself! Some of these stories might have been true, but I have no way of predicting the future and knowing which ones. Also, if I had allowed my mind to go there, I would have missed out on enjoying the rest of my walk because I would have been worrying incessantly about something I can't even control. My focus on simply enjoying the walk we were taking allowed me instead to be in the moment and enjoy the time I do have with Einstein."

In addition to being sloppy and loud, the third problem with self-talk is that it can sometimes increase our suffering in life. We talked about how self-talk often develops into patterns, many of which are negative in some way. As we engage in these patterns, they can hugely impact our overall attitude and experience. Simply imagine that we had a friend who constantly criticized everything with us 24 hours a day. Clearly, this would be a downer. In truth, even having this friend with us five or ten minutes every hour would impact our attitude and outlook toward life. In fact, we'd be so overly focused on the negative elements of our lives, we might miss out on the good entirely. Although this criticalness is true for some people's self-talk more than others, it can definitely be a problem.

Overall, then, self-talk has its pluses and minuses. It represents a mental shorthand that we need, but it makes sloppy judgments that are often negative, loud, and verbose. Ideally, we'd like to keep the swiftness of our assessments while turning down the volume, quantity, and negativity. Sound too good to be true? In fact, this turns out to be entirely possible. We can intentionally replace the negative with positive *and* significantly decrease the volume and quantity of our self-talk. We'll give you tools to make these changes in the next couple of chapters. The first step, however, is simply recognizing our current self-talk and the pluses and minuses it provides for us.

Putting It into Practice

To review, self-talk is the internal commentary that happens in our minds. It consists of thoughts about both internal and external factors; in other words, we commentate on both ourselves and others. We have thoughts about what we like or don't like, how we (or others) look or behave, what happened earlier today, and more. In fact, we often even have thoughts about our thoughts themselves (e.g., "well that's a stupid idea"). We all have this self-talk, although it may vary in its valence (i.e., positive or negative), intensity, and degree of elaboration. Self-talk ranges from quick chit-chat to the elaborate stories we hear in our minds.

Self-talk originates from an early age as we interact with important others and form opinions about the world. It tends to develop into themes and patterns of thinking that continue throughout our lives. While these themes and patterns help us to make quick assessments, they also create a few problems. First, they simply make sloppy mistakes. Second, self-talk often makes us miss out on our moment-to-moment experience because it's so loud and verbose, taking up all of our attention. Third, self-talk often consists of negative patterns that drastically color our experience of life. Because of these downsides to self-talk, it becomes critical for us to turn down the volume, quantity, and negativity of it in our minds. Just like turning down a radio dial, this is how we quiet the critic in our minds. We make the commentary a soft background noise that we can tune into when we want, and we can tune out of when it's not helpful.

As we've said, the first step in turning down our self-talk is actually tuning into it enough to figure out what's going on in our minds. In other words, we have to figure out how much self-talk we currently have, how loud it is, what it's about, etc. Remember, the first step toward change is always increasing our awareness of our current circumstances. Hence, take a few moments right now to sit quietly and simply tune into your self-talk. The best way to do this is to write down (as quickly as you can) all of the thoughts that run through your head for two minutes. Set a timer before you start and then simply let your mind roam freely. Try your best to simply notice your thoughts, without directing or critiquing them in any way. When you're ready, record your self-talk here:

Questions for Reflection

1) How easy or difficult was it for me to simply sit quietly and notice my thoughts?

2) What is the quality of my thoughts? In other words, do they seem quiet or loud, benign or critical, simple or elaborate?

3) As I read back over my thoughts, do I notice any patterns (e.g., critiquing, planning, sulking, praising)?

4) Do I notice any themes in my thoughts (e.g., thoughts about my kids, work, etc.)?

5) Based on these reflections, how does my self-talk impact me positively or negatively? Does it create sloppy mistakes, make me miss out on my moment-to-moment experience, or put a negative tone to my life?

Tip #5: Remember to Say "Please" and "Thank You"

Most of us learned to say "please" and "thank you" in kindergarten. This lesson was sandwiched between the lessons on how to cut along a line with scissors and how to spell our own name. Clearly, these latter lessons are pretty well-engrained. For some reason, however, we seem to have more trouble with the first lesson—remembering to say "please" and "thank you."

And, no, we're not just talking about talking about saying "please" or "thank you" as you check out from the grocery store or receive some other service. While that may be important, we're talking about a broader sense of openness and gratitude in life. We're talking about living with a sense of desire, expectation, and gratitude rather than one of entitlement. This is really where we seem to have lost our "please" and "thank you's"—in our overall stance toward living.

In order to experience health and happiness in our minds, we must re-learn how to live with openness and gratitude rather than entitlement. We must let go of our sense that we *deserve* a new car or the latest cell phone. We must unclench our hands of all those "shoulds" and "musts" that plague us in our lives—e.g., "I should be treated by everyone around me with respect," "I must have everything that my friends or neighbors have." In this chapter, we'll talk about the importance and power of making this shift from entitlement to openness and gratitude.

The Power of Perspective

Gratitude is a powerful force. It's also one that's been well-researched in a movement referred to as "positive psychology." This research has shown that gratitude both contributes to our well-being and buffers us against the negative effects of stress.[ii] In fact, people who are grateful have been shown to experience greater life satisfaction and decreased rates of burnout.[iii] Gratitude also appears to foster social support.[iv] In other words, it appears that gratitude connects us to others; helps us to experience more happiness in life; and protects us from depression, burnout, and other results of stress.

Gratitude is an amazing gift that stands in stark contrast to the "give-me-more" attitude of entitlement. When we're grateful, we're thankful for what we have. We may desire more, but we're able to feel happy where we are and patiently wait for new things. In contrast, entitlement involves an expectation that I *should* have more—and have it *NOW*. Because of this expectation, we're often unable to fully enjoy what we do have in the present. Overall, entitlement is greedy and close-fisted, whereas gratitude tends to hold loosely and give generously with open hands. Most importantly, gratitude and entitlement are different attitudes—not circumstances.

Dr. White: "When I completed my doctorate in psychology, I came face to face with my own feelings of entitlement. It was a tough economy and, in spite of having multiple employers who wanted to hire me, I couldn't find a single one with the funds. I applied to everything I could find for over eight months and eventually had to settle on multiple, low-paying, part-time jobs to try and pay some bills while continuing to move forward in my career. I worked late almost every evening, creating quite a tax on my family. Meanwhile, I made 1/3 to 1/2 of the salary that I was making in my job *before* grad school. Guess what? I was pissed. After a career change and six years in graduate school, I felt entitled to have a job…even a well-paying job—and preferably one that I loved! I was frustrated, angry, and probably pretty negative. After awhile, it was hard to even hope in things changing, and I spent some time fighting regret over my choice to go to graduate school. I hate to admit it, but I was not in a very good place in terms or my attitude or perspective on life. After about eight months, I finally gave up. I let go of my entitlement, surrendered to what was, and began trying to accept the present. Miraculously, I began to find things to be grateful for again. I also began to encounter all kinds of opportunities I hadn't noticed before—including writing my first e-book. Although I still had a lot of long days and tough moments, I felt more positive and hopeful overall. In fact, nine months later, I even turned down a well-paying, full-time job because I realized that I enjoyed what I was doing. Buy why? My circumstances hadn't changed. What had? The one thing I had control over—my attitude and perspective. I had shifted from feeling entitled and focusing on what I wanted (and didn't have) to feeling grateful for what was actually before me."

As Dr. White's story illustrates, gratitude is an attitude that opens us to enjoying our lives, whereas entitlement is one that instead obsesses on what we don't have (and think we should). And surprisingly, it is actually our choice whether we are grateful or entitled. While it might appear that gratitude and entitlement flow directly from our circumstances, the truth is that our attitude is simply a matter of perspective. We can choose to look at our circumstances with either gratitude or entitlement, reaping the amazing benefits of the former or experiencing the embittering consequences of the latter.

Making a Mental Shift

So how do we make the shift to embracing gratitude over entitlement? The most important step is disciplining our minds to focus on the things we have and appreciate. The truth is that we get to choose what we focus on, and our focus shapes our attitude. For example, do we focus on what's missing in our lives, or what we have and like? There was a vast difference in Dr. White's overall perspective when she focused on the wonderful opportunities and supportive husband she did have, rather than the full-time, well-paying job she didn't. Shifting our attitude is all about shifting our mental focus.

> *Dr. Puff:* "As I look back on my life, I can clearly see the importance of mental focus. I recall making the conscious choice in my 20's that I would focus on the positive. I began filling my drive to work with positive CDs, leaving myself affirming notes, and even placing note cards with positive sayings around my house. I intentionally read and meditated upon positive things about myself and the world. It was amazing the difference this made. As I shifted from allowing my surroundings to fill my mind—usually with lots of negative things, like the world news—to intentionally filling them with the positive, I noticed a significant (and lasting) shift in my attitude and mood. My negative thought patterns were replaced with positive ones, and this opened the door for me to simply live each day and enjoy it for what it is."

Clearly, our focus is important and can vastly shift our perspective. If we focus on what might go wrong (or, perhaps, did yesterday), we're likely to tell ourselves stories of past or future calamity. Similarly, if we focus on what is wrong with today, we'll probably experience frustration and perhaps even bitterness or depression as we rehash negative stories. In contrast, if we instead focus on what simply is—or better yet, is good—today, we can minimize these negative stories and actually enjoy the present. Shifting our focus can drastically change our attitude.

Shifting our focus changes our attitude because it shapes how we see and experience things. Let's consider a simple example. Imagine a single woman who desperately wants to be married and have a family. If this woman focuses on her lack of family, she might wake up every morning feeling frustrated that she is alone. She'd probably also notice every love song on the radio and couple or family on the street with heightened sensitivities. Her focus on what she didn't have would likely increase her misery over being single. If, however, this woman instead held her desire for a family a little more loosely and allowed herself to enjoy the time that she was single, she might notice opportunities to get involved in evening activities with friends or volunteer groups that she wouldn't have time for as a wife and mom. While these things might not replace her desire for family, they would likely provide joy and satisfaction in the present until the time was right for that change. Clearly, our focus impacts what we notice in our daily lives and how we experience these things.

So is this an easy or quick change? Unfortunately, it's probably more slow and gradual for most people. Making a mental shift to the positive involves many steps. First we notice our current thoughts. We may assess whether they are positive, negative, or someplace in between. We may also ask ourselves questions like, "Are these thoughts true?" and "Are they necessary?" Many of Dr. Puff's negative thoughts were probably not true and did not deserve his time and attention. Many of the single woman's thoughts about wanting a family are true, but they still aren't a necessary (or helpful) focus for all of her attention. Once we decide something isn't true or necessary, it may be easier to make the shift and replace the thought with something more positive.

It is important to make one point of clarification here: Focusing on what is—or what is good—about today does not mean thinking everything is perfect all the time. Things may indeed be difficult or even painful. We don't pretend this isn't the case. Instead, we do our best to focus on what is good and trust that things will work out for the best in the end. This is the perspective of an aegethist. It falls between a pessimist, who believes everything is negative, and an optimist, who believes everything is good. An aegethist instead believes that some things are good and some aren't, but all things will work out in the end. As a result, an aegethist is able to have an open perspective that has preferences but can also accept and—most of the time—even love what is.

Putting It into Practice

Overall, this is good news: We can choose what we focus on, and our focus will directly impact our attitude. We will have times of lack and difficulty in our lives, and it's important to deal with those things. However, if we choose to dwell on what we have and appreciate, trusting that even the hard things will work out in the end, we are likely to notice and experience the opportunities and goodness in our lives. Instead of feeling the bitterness of entitlement, we will experience the powerful gift of gratitude. It's truly a matter of perspective—not circumstance, flowing directly out of where we choose to put our focus.

This is why it's critical to remember to say our "please" and "thank you's." As we say these words, we not only put goodness out into the world—we experience it on ourselves. We begin to feel grateful and enjoy what is. Although it's not more complicated in theory than cutting with scissors or spelling our names correctly, this shift is powerful. It turns out our kindergarten teachers were right—saying "please" and "thank you" are pretty important after all.

Ready to say some "please" and "thank you's" now? Here's the challenge: Take a few minutes to thoughtfully make a list of *at least ten* things that you are grateful for. Each of these things must reflect your current circumstances—not something that used to be or might be in the future. Each of them will hopefully stand alone too; in other words, it's important not to follow them up by some sort of "but" or caveat. So we can be thankful for having a roof over our heads. Period. We want to try to avoid listing the house we used to own or might move into next month. We also want to avoid following thankfulness for a roof over our heads with "even though I live with my parents." Each item should stand-alone as something we are thankful for in our lives today. Make your list here:

1) ______________________________________

____

____

2) ______________________________

____

____

3) ______________________________

____

____

4) ______________________________

____

____

5) ______________________________

____

____

6) ______________________________

____

____

7) ______________________________

____

____

8) ______________________________

____

____

9) ______________________________

____

____

10) ______________________________

____

____

Now, take the next 24 hours to read through your list. Schedule appointed times when you will read and really think about it at least five times over these 24 hours. You may set reminders on your calendar to read it first thing in the morning, when you get to work, during lunch, when you leave work, and before you go to bed. Alternatively, you may simply tie the activity to something you are already doing multiple times a day, such as eating, drinking, or using the restroom. Whatever the schedule, be intentional to follow through with reading and meditating on your list at least five times over 24 hours. Then complete the questions for reflection.

Questions for Reflection

1) How difficult was it for me to make a list of things I'm grateful for?

2) Was it easy or hard for me to remember to read through my list throughout the day?

3) Based on my answers to the first two questions, is gratitude something that seems to come easily for me, or something that creates more of a challenge?

4) How did making and reading through my list impact my attitude or experience of the day?

5) Are there any ways I'd like to more permanently institute an intentional focus on gratitude into my daily life?

Tip #6: Be Still and Know that I Am

Many people in the Judeo-Christian tradition are familiar with the Psalm which asks us to "Be still, and know that I am God" (Psalm 46:10). Regardless of one's religious perspective, we've learned that these words contain a lot of wisdom. It is crucial for us to simply be still and, well, just be. Whether we do this by ourselves or with others (divine or not!), the stance of simply being is critical to our health and success.

This idea of simply "being" may sound bizarre to many people because it is a pretty counter-cultural idea. We are much more accustomed to *doing* than *being.* Other than when we're asleep, we tend to be a culture on the go, moving from one activity to the next. Even within each of those activities, we're often focused on the next thing we have to do rather than the one we are currently doing. Let's face it—we are a culture driven by movement and activity.

While movement and activity aren't bad, a life of only *doing* tends to be exhausting and, ironically, pretty empty. *Being* allows us to connect to a deeper part of ourselves, others, life, and even God. Being also creates a stillness and presence inside of us that allows us to notice and engage in our lives more—even when we are *doing.* Being is a critical aspect of our lives. In this chapter, we'll introduce you to meditation, which is a proven way to grow our ability to simply be.

Meditation: Weird, Religious Tradition or Wisdom of the Ages?

Meditation originates from Eastern philosophies and traditions. As a result, some of us may hear the word "meditation" and imagine some weird, out-of-touch, ancient, religious practice. While understandable, many of these reactions probably reveal more about our biases toward things we don't understand than they do about meditation.

Interestingly, meditation has taken much of the West by storm in the last 40 years. Why? Because it's a powerful activity that holds many benefits for those who practice. In fact, research has shown that meditation can reduce insomnia,[v] stress,[vi] burn out,[vii] pain,[viii] and depression relapse.[ix] At the same time, meditation can improve attention[x], memory,[xi] immune system functioning,[xii] and overall well-being.[vii] Even from this small sampling of research, it's clear that the benefits of meditation are numerous and diverse.

Dr. Puff: "I've been meditating for over 30 years. During this time, I've seen meditation move me from a place of worrying and striving to one of peace and presence. I've really come to a place where I can live the phrase, 'Accept what is, love what is.' I have desires and goals, but I really live and work out of a place of enjoying what I do and where I'm at now. As a result, I'm less attached to specific outcomes and I can be flexible and embrace what actually happens. I'm also able to enjoy it even more because

I have a quietness to my mind that simply allows me to be present with the moment-to-moment experience of my day. In addition, I regularly have pretty awe-inspiring, transcendent experiences connected to my meditation practice. Above all, though, I feel like meditation has given me a sense that all is well with the world and my life."

Whether we turn to research or our personal experience, it's true: Meditation can provide us immense benefits. What's more, these benefits truly span the physical, cognitive, emotional, relational, and even spiritual realms. We can think of very few other things that boast such broad benefits. And, amazingly, meditation can do all of this without any particular religious or spiritual affiliation. Clearly, the East has passed along an immensely wise and powerful *human* practice.

Meditation: What It Is…and What It's Not

Having said all that, meditation may still sound pretty mystical to many people. What exactly is it? Meditation is basically a type of mental exercise that engages us in stillness. Although it is possible to walk or do some other activity while meditating, most people usually sit comfortably and quietly. While sitting, meditators focus on the in and out of their breath or some other quiet, soothing sound (e.g., soft music, a short phrase or "mantra"). Sometimes meditators visualize a calm place or check in with their bodies, but usually they just try to be. Meditation is an exercise in ceasing activity and simply being still.

When many people hear this, they think meditation is about clearing their minds. They still want to *do* something, so they focus on trying to stop their thoughts. This is not meditation. Practicing meditation regularly does tend to slow our thoughts down (and sometimes halt them briefly, like a wave that has just crashed on the shore), but our thoughts never permanently cease. Our thoughts are normal and inevitable—even good, actually, as they mean our brains are still working! Rather than trying to clear our thoughts, we simply notice them as we meditate. It's like laying down and watching the clouds pass by; we are not any one cloud and we don't need to get stuck on any one cloud—we just notice them float by. Our thoughts don't cease in meditation, but they do decrease as we become less caught up in them.

We are able to become less caught up in our thoughts because meditation opens the door for us to be more mindful. Mindfulness is a closely related concept and practice to meditation. Mindfulness emphasizes two things: First, engagement in the present moment, and, second, non-judgment. So as we meditate or become mindful, we become fully engaged in this moment, right now. Our awareness increases—just as we discussed in the "Gaze Into the Looking Glass" chapter. We may notice our surroundings and ourselves (e.g., our thoughts, feelings, physical sensations) with new eyes. Although this can take a lot of practice, ideally we are aware in a way that notices without judging. We notice the "clouds" (or sensations, feelings, circumstances, etc.) without deciding if they are good or bad, right or wrong. This combination of nonjudgmental awareness allows us to experience greater peace, presence, and acceptance of our lives as they are right now.

> *Dr. White:* "Although my meditation practice is newer than Dr. Puff's, I've noticed many benefits too. My mind has definitely slowed down. Even when I'm really busy, I feel like I'm walking briskly through life rather than running, which is much less exhausting and harried. I also feel a greater sense of peace, acceptance, and even joy with my life as it is now. I still have goals and dreams that I'd like to accomplish, but I am engaged and happy in today...with a whole lot less pressure. Of course, today still has challenges at times; even then, however, my meditation and mindfulness helps me to tolerate and learn from the challenges rather than become overwhelmed by them. Meditating even 10-20 minutes per day is a huge gift to myself of presence and peace."

As Dr. White's story illustrates, meditation does not preclude goal-setting or dreaming. We still think about and plan for the future; actually, we are generally able to do this in a much more focused way as a result of the clarity of mind that comes with meditation. Hopefully, we also still think about and process the past when it's relevant and important. The difference is that in spite of thinking about the future and processing the past, *we are increasingly living in the present.* Meditation allows us to use our thoughts and minds as a tool to help us live well…without allowing them to run us from one activity and "what if" to the next all day long. Meditation also allows us a sense of peace, presence, and awe in the world. Overall, then, meditation is simply an exercise of being still that allows us to connect more deeply to ourselves and our lives, creating all kinds of benefits both in and out of that moment.

Don't Wait!

Before we move on to issuing the challenge of actually trying meditation, it's important to address one major objection: "I don't have time right now because of ____________ *(you fill in the blank)*." In our fast-paced, activity-driven world, we often struggle to make time for relaxation and rest. Going to the extreme of actually stopping and being still may seem almost ridiculous in the midst of this struggle. Shouldn't we just wait until we finish school, our kids get a little older, or our job slows down?? The answer is a resounding, *NO!* We cannot wait until our lives slow down to make space for ourselves or our health.

The problem with waiting until our lives finally "slow down" is that they never do—or at least not for long. As soon as we finish one thing, something else arises to take its place. Yes, we have probably accomplished something significant in the process—like finishing school, landing that promotion, or buying that new toy—but, like it or not, the happiness, relief, and peace that follow are usually short-lived. We rarely (if ever!) actually "arrive" to this mythical place of *lasting* happiness, space, and rest. What rest and space we do find—like those one week vacations we eek out every year or two—never seems to last long enough. Whether we are busting our behinds trying to finish school, get that promotion, buy that new toy, or whatever else is on our list, most likely we will never "arrive" to that place of rest and space that we imagine.

In reality, this mentality of "waiting to arrive" is an example of "delay of gratification" gone awry. "Delay of gratification" refers to skipping or postponing a pleasure now in order to accomplish something or have a greater pleasure later. Our parents force us to start this process early when they require us to eat our lima beans before we can have ice cream. We forgo the pleasure of throwing our lima beans in the trash so that we can enjoy that Rocky Road. This is great as long as we do enjoy the ice cream eventually.

But imagine another scenario for a moment: Let's say we finish our lima beans, only to have our mother place another helping on our plate, stating that our first serving was too small. After glaring at her, we eat our second serving of lima beans...only to have her place a *third* serving on our plate. Sound ridiculous? In theory it is ridiculous, yet we do it to ourselves all the time.

The truth is that we have a tendency to allow our goals and plans to supersede living and loving life, right here and right now. We tell ourselves, "Someday I'll slow down. Someday I'll enjoy life, but right now I need to ______ (*what fills in the blank for you?*). When I reach my goals, then I'll slow down and enjoy life." That plan would never be ideal, but it might be okay if we really stuck to it. The problem is that most of us have already set new goals (or are behind on old ones) by the time we finish our first set of goals. Do we take time to celebrate and set a new pace for life? Nope, we delay enjoying life again, telling ourselves it really will be different next time. If we're not careful, it can literally become a life of all lima beans! We may entirely and permanently miss today because we are so focused on "arriving" at some mythical destination.

Unfortunately, in addition to missing today because we are so focused on arriving, this way of living often creates some significant problems for us along the way too. While we are working our behinds off, trying to accomplish some important goal, we tend to overly focus on one or maybe two areas of our lives. We often develop our professional muscles, yet we ignore our emotional or relational muscles. Or perhaps we manage to squeeze in one important relationship, yet ignore our physical and spiritual muscles. As long as we stay in the professional realm, this may work okay—assuming our other muscles aren't so atrophied they start creating other problems, like heart disease or relationship meltdowns. Even if this isn't the case, as soon as we get thrown into another area of life—like having kids or dealing with grief—we're in trouble. We simply haven't developed enough muscles to be successful in those areas.

While it's tempting and pretty normal to live in this imbalanced way, the truth is that very few of us find real, lasting happiness or peace narrowly focusing on one area of our lives. This isn't any more successful for us than waiting to arrive. So does this mean we stop setting goals and working hard? Absolutely not! It's great to set goals and work hard. Sometimes we may even give ourselves permission to have *short seasons* that are slightly out of balance. As a whole, however, we have to stop waiting and start living the lives we want now. Waiting brings a life of lima beans, while living now allows us to balance those lima beans with the Rocky Road or other things we crave—creating more enjoyment and health along the way.

Putting It into Practice

We can begin creating more health and pleasure in our lives *today* through the practice of meditation. Meditation is an ancient wisdom that calls us to simply be still, focusing on our breath or some other gentle stimuli, and just noticing what's present—both inside and around us. We can tell you from research and from our own personal experience that meditation is a simple idea which definitely packs a punch. We can also tell you from our personal experience that the perfect time to slow down will never "arrive"...and yet we can each choose to make the time today.

Why? Because we need balance in our lives. As challenging as it may be, it's critical that we balance the lima beans with the Rocky Road (and every other important food group!). Balance is a definite theme of this book, and here we are applying it specifically to our minds. We can balance our minds by creating time for stillness and simply "being" in the midst of all the planning, judging, thinking, etc. we use our minds for all day long. Although it may sound counter-cultural, this really isn't a new idea; it dates all the way back to the Judeo-Christian idea of simply being still, remembering that we are first human beings (not human doings!), who are not an island unto ourselves.

So let's get started. For this activity, it's important that you find a quiet place, free from as many distractions as possible. Definitely turn off the TV and preferably silence any electronic devices. Then allow yourself to sit comfortably. If sitting is uncomfortable due to pain or other issues, it is possible (although less desirable due to fatigue) to meditate while laying down. If you've never meditated before, set a timer for about 5-10 minutes (longer is even better, but this will probably feel like an eternity the first time).

After finishing these instructions, close your eyes and simply notice the slow inhalation and exhalation of your breath. Also, try silently repeating the phrase "I am peaceful" with each breath ("I am" on the inhalation and "peaceful" on the exhalation). Do this until the timer goes off. Yes, your mind will wander. That's okay; when you notice it wandering, simply return to your breath and the phrase "I am peaceful." When you're done, take a minute or two just to open your eyes and re-acclimate to your surroundings; then move on to the questions for reflection.

Questions for Reflection

1) What was my first reaction to reading about stillness and meditation? Are these ideas which generally appeal to me and fit my life, or do they seem like quite a stretch and challenge?

2) How did I feel before starting the meditation?

3) Was it easy or difficult to enter into this activity?

4) What did I notice during meditation? For example, were my thoughts incessant and active? Did the time feel like forever? Did I notice any feelings or physical sensations in my body?

5) How did I feel when I finished the meditation? Were there any changes from my answer in question #2?

Note: For further practice with meditation, refer to Dr. Puff's free meditation podcasts at www.meditationforhealthpodcast.com.

Tying It All Together

Whether we attend to it or not, there is a lot of important activity happening in the mind. First off, we all have an abundance of self-talk. Self-talk is the thoughts, or internal commentary, that happen in our minds. It includes thoughts about both ourselves and others, and it can range in intensity from idle chit-chat to elaborate stories. Our self-talk provides some significant benefits in helping us to make quick assessments about life, but it also makes a lot of sloppy mistakes and can become so loud that we miss out on the moment we are actually living. Because of the difficulties that self-talk can create, it's important to increase our awareness of it and even *quiet the critic* or commentator that resides there.

We work to quiet the critic because where we place our focus matters. In fact, our focus directly impacts our attitude and experience of life. Our self-talk tends to develop into patterns of thinking which drive our focus to some things more than others. These patterns and the resulting focus can then create an attitude of entitlement and bitterness or one of gratitude. Whichever way our focus takes us, our attitude will follow and directly impact our experience of life—as much or more as the actual circumstances. As a result, we do ourselves a huge favor by training our minds to focus on the positive, feeling grateful for and enjoying what is. Although this training can be difficult, it often begins with simply *remembering to say our "please" and "thank you's."*

As we train our minds by directing our self-talk toward the positive, we can also train our minds through meditation. Meditation is an ancient wisdom that calls us to simply be still, focusing on our breath or some other gentle stimuli, and just noticing what's present—both inside and around us. As we engage our minds in this way, we create space for stillness and being in the midst of all the busy activity. We are able to simply *be still and know that we are*—aside from anything that does or does not get done on our "to do" list today.

There are many components of the minds, most of which we often taken for granted. Like it or not, however, each and every one of these pieces—from our self-talk, or thoughts, to our attitude and the activity level of our mind—has an impact on our well-being. And, like the professional dancer, we will perform much better when we can harness these varying aspects into a focus that allows us to be positively present in the moment of the performance. How do we do this? First we become aware of the self-talk, attitudes, and activity level currently happening in our minds. Then we gradually make the shift from negative to positive and loud to quiet. Gratitude can be an immensely helpful tool in making the first shift, and meditation can help with the second. As we employ these tools, we, too, can soon be dancing through life with the focus of a spontaneous child and trained expert.

Part III: Body

It goes without saying that a great dancer must keep up her body. Since her work and art are embodied activities, there is no debate or wiggle-room here. For young children, this tends to come pretty naturally (or at least it did until the advent of video and computer games!). For adults, it usually requires a lot of discipline and effort. Many of us would love to have the physique of adult, professional dancers…without all this work! We'd love to have a healthy body naturally and spontaneously—like a child who stays healthy without thought or effort.

Interestingly, we find that it is necessary to combine the natural tendencies of the child with the discipline of the adult to create something that works here. For most of us, it isn't enough to simply leave it to chance like the child. We have to discipline ourselves enough to at least develop some healthy physical habits. However, as we will discuss more in the upcoming chapters, we will fail in this discipline if it isn't organic and enjoyable like the child. Hence, succeeding in the physical realm requires a combination of the free, abandoned child with the disciplined and skilled professional.

Before we go on, allow us to acknowledge that a lot of people bring a lot of "knowledge" and baggage into this area. We've all heard a lot about nutrition, exercise, and stress, so we think we know it all. Ironically, this is true even if we fail time and time again to achieve the diet, activity, or stress level we desire. If that's the case, we may feel a lot of frustration or even shame, and wish someone would wave a magic wand that grants us the body and health we've always desired—not tell us more about these topics! We understand that talking about the body can stir up a lot of reactions, including some pretty intense emotions and even aversions.

In spite of that, we encourage readers to stick with us. We actually have some fairly uncommon things to say in each of these areas—things which might actually help each of us to find the success we've always wanted with our bodies. And, yes, this does matter. Our body is the vehicle that takes us through life. When it functions well, we have a much better chance of finding success with our minds, hearts, and relationships. When, in contrast, our bodies are unhealthy, we'll simply never find the success we are really looking for in life. This area, like it or not, can make or break us. As a result, this section will talk about each of these "old" physical emphases in new ways, hopefully invigorating new life and success into our physical journeys.

Tip #7: Just Enjoy It!

We've all heard that famous advertising slogan, "Just do it." There is probably a lot of wisdom in this statement for many things in life. Sometimes we have to just dive in and go back to school, look for a new job, or even take a risk in a relationship. Hopefully we're discerning, thoughtful, and seeking wise counsel in these decisions, but there does sometimes come a point where we just have to move forward—in spite of ongoing fears or other hesitations. Sometimes it does make sense to, "Just do it."

Having said all that, we don't believe that exercise is one of those times to, "Just do it." Yes, let us first acknowledge that we just used the "E" word, which may frighten or simply turn off a lot of people. Hang in there with us for a minute because you may find we have something new to say on this topic. Exercise is critical for the body and the brain. We're actually amazed at the increasing research which shows how much exercise impacts our health on all levels. We'll talk a little more about that as we move forward, but first, let us acknowledge: Exercise is not something most of us can successfully *push through* for our entire lives. Exercise is not something we can "just do" day in and day out.

How do we know this? We know it because large chunks of the population are continually resolving (every January, in fact) to "just do" their workouts…only to fail and give up, generally within a pretty short period of time. It's hard. We can force ourselves to "just do" something for a relatively short period of time. We can push ourselves into taking the plunge or sucking it up for the day. We are NOT successful, however, at pushing ourselves to do something we hate day in and day out. Eventually, our preferences override our willpower and we stop "just doing it."

So does this mean we just give up and choose a different New Years' Resolution? Not necessarily. There is a little talked about alternative to "just doing" (or giving up entirely on) exercise. We can make it something we actually enjoy. After all, aren't we able to continually watch our favorite TV shows, spend time with friends we like, and maintain other things we genuinely enjoy? What if working out could be an enjoyable activity as well? In this chapter, we'll discuss why exercise is important as well as a variety of ways to maintain it through enjoyment.

Exercise: Gym Teachers' "Should" or Real Wisdom?

Before we talk about how to make exercise something we can enjoy, it's important to stop and consider whether it's really all that critical after all. Is exercise actually essential to our health, or is it one of those little things our high school gym teacher and perhaps grandma passed down as important with no basis in reality? This is a fair question to ask. Sadly, the answer we've come up with is, *"No—exercise is not some archaic idea we can throw out."*

Like it or not, exercise actually turns out to be pretty critical to our health. As we know, exercise helps us to keep our bodies healthy. For example, cardio activity improves our heart health, and stretching improves our flexibility. Of course, exercise is also helpful for maintaining our weight. In addition, regular exercise increases our energy levels throughout the day. Clearly, exercise is good for our physical health.

Fortunately or unfortunately, though, the benefits of exercise go far beyond our physical health. For example, recent research has found that exercise, ranging from aerobic to stretching, has positive effects on memory for middle-aged adults.[xiii] Research has also shown that exercise decreases stress, anxiety, and depression—again, regardless of the intensity of the workout.[xiv] Many other studies have supported both cognitive and psychological benefits for exercise.[xv, xvi, xvii] Some studies have also extended the results to children, showing that exercise helps kids to think more clearly and do better in school.[xviii] Like it or not—for any age and body type—exercise does much more than keep our bodies healthy.

It's true: Exercise is a huge component of our physical, cognitive, and emotional health. It doesn't just keep our bodies in shape—exercise also keeps our minds in shape and our emotions in check. Some experts have even suggested that exercise and other, positive health behaviors can actually slow the impact of aging—again, both physically and cognitively. It's time to admit it: Our gym teacher was right on this one. Anyone who's concerned with their physical, cognitive, or emotional health should look into exercising!

Trash the Misconceptions

As we consider "looking into" exercise, it's important to note what may be deterring us from it. We tend to have a lot of beliefs about what exercise is and what it's not that keep us struck in cycles of effort and failure. For example, a lot of us believe (consciously or unconsciously) that exercise has to be unpleasant. This is simply not true. We're willing to bet there have been at least a few times in all of our lives that we enjoyed some physical activity—whether it be a walk on the beach during a relaxing vacation or a romp in the sheets with our spouse. These physical activities burned calories and did our body good, just like any run on the treadmill—even though we probably didn't stop to think about them as exercise. As long as we keep believing exercise has to be unpleasant, however, we are doomed to do things we hate and cannot sustain.

We'll talk in a moment about how to shift this pattern. But first, what are other beliefs that keep sabotaging our attempts at exercise? Here are a few:

**Exercise has to be painful and make me sweat.* This is simply not true. As we mentioned above, there are a lot of important types of exercise, including strength training and flexibility. Getting our heart rate up is important at times, but it isn't the whole story. It also doesn't have to be high intensity (i.e., sweating profusely and exhausting) to benefit our hearts.

**Exercise has to happen at the gym.* This is a pretty insidious idea. We don't realize we believe it, yet the gym is where we often start our resolutions…even if we hate it there! The truth is that exercise can happen in our neighborhoods, homes, or even work. Really, any place we have the space to move, we can exercise.

**Exercise has to happen all at once.* How many times do we start our resolutions by trying to carve out large chunks of time everyday for exercise? Talk about difficult! No wonder we can't sustain it. The truth is that exercise can also occur in small chunks of time throughout the day. One study even tested differing lengths of exercise time and recommended that adults engage in just 30 minutes of moderate activity daily—but accumulated in shorter chunks throughout the day![xv]

**Exercise has to be expensive.* This is another one that we use as a good excuse to not exercise—"I can't afford it." Wrong again! Exercise does not have to involve a gym membership, expensive equipment, or any other large expenses. Yes, it can if we have the resources and would enjoy those things. However, if we can't afford it or wouldn't enjoy it, we can just as easily throw on a pair of tennis shoes and go walk around the block.

All of these beliefs about exercise are common and wrong. Exercise does not have to be expensive, painful, or unpleasant. It also doesn't have to consist of large chunks of time at the gym. In fact, we'll discuss some of the alternatives for the rest of the chapter. For now, though, we hope that exposing and confronting these myths gets us all thinking a little bit. Our list of misconceptions is by no means exhaustive, yet it reveals what a narrow box we often place exercise in…dooming it to failure. It's time now to trash these misconceptions and open our minds to something new—something which may actually lead us to success in an area of constant struggle.

Find Something Enjoyable

As we open our minds to new possibilities for exercise, let's start by thinking about activities we might actually enjoy. For those who do enjoy running on the treadmill at the gym, fantastic! For the rest of us, let's get creative. First, think about what types of activities have been enjoyable in the past, even if we didn't consider them exercise at the time. For example, many people enjoy bowling on the Wii or other active video games. Others might enjoy moments of spontaneous dancing…without ever having thought about pumping the music and letting lose as a workout. The best place to start with exercise is thinking about physical activities we already enjoy or might like to try.

The second step in finding physical activities we enjoy is combining them with other things we like. For instance, perhaps we enjoy time outside and with friends. If so, a good exercise choice might be walking in the park with a buddy; even if the walking doesn't thrill us, we may find we really enjoy the time because it provides us space to enjoy other things we like. Alternatively, perhaps we really enjoy competition. If so, challenging our friends to a "who can work out more" week on Facebook might add the thrill to our activities. Finding things we enjoy that we can pair with physical activity may turn up our enjoyment of exercise even more.

> *Dr. Puff*: "I do a variety of physical activities on a daily and weekly basis because I enjoy them. I walk, do yoga, and even lift weights. I've found that these are things which benefit me—body and soul. I've also found ways to turn up the enjoyment by pairing these activities with other things I like. For example, I usually take my dog out and go hiking with an audio book. Now, my 'exercise' has turned into a blast with four things I enjoy—walking, nature, my dog, and books. It may take a little experimentation, but finding things we enjoy makes exercise a blessing rather than a burden in the end."

Dr. Puff's comments illustrate our end goal: Making exercise a blessing rather than a burden. Simply imagine that exercise could be something that one looked forward to and missed when it didn't happen, rather than something that was dreaded on a daily basis. We know this is possible because we've both experienced it. To get there, start by creatively thinking outside the box. What activities are enjoyable, and how can they be combined with other fun things to turn up the pleasure even more?

Mix It Up!

Another key to making exercise enjoyable is *variety*. Some people can be satisfied doing the same activity every day for the rest of their lives; they probably already work out consistently. For the rest of us, we simply get sick of things—even things we enjoy. We may also find that certain activities fit our lifestyle for awhile and then we need to make adjustments as the season of our life changes. This is normal and okay. The important thing is to adjust accordingly and mix it up every now and then.

Dr. White: "I've been working out consistently for well over ten years. I admit that I started out by sheer self-discipline, jogging everyday because I bought into the myth that I had to work hard and be in pain for my workout to be worthwhile. Since then, I've evolved a lot in my thinking (and doing) of exercise. Now I can honestly say I exercise 4-5 times a week because I enjoy it. How do I keep the enjoyment alive? I mix it up based on what sounds good and fits my season of life. Over the last 10+ years this has included quite a variety: Jogging, walking, swimming, biking, kick-boxing, stepping and other aerobic classes, playing active video games (DDR is still a favorite), busting a move with workout videos (love Paula Abdul's dance video especially), jump roping, hiking, personal training, doing yoga and more. I've worked out alone and in large groups; for awhile, I even had a group of about 15 students from around the globe doing Tae Bo in our school basement. I've exercised at home, at the gym, and all kinds of place outside. I've also varied my workouts from a 20 minute run on busy days to 2 hour training sessions for a triathalon. Lest this sound impressive, let me also add that I do not have an athletic bone in my body. The difference has simply been getting creative and mixing it up so that I could find regular workouts that are doable and enjoyable for me."

Dr. White's comments illustrate the importance of variety in our exercise. For most of us, variety makes it more enjoyable and more doable. Variety also allows us to think outside of the box and get creative. For example, we might vacuum and clean with vigor to turn our chores for the day into a moderate intensity workout. Some people also get a lot of mileage out of making things like errands or bathroom breaks into short walks by purposely walking (or even taking the stairs) to the farthest restroom or parking spot. With a little creativity, it's actually quite easy (and usually not very time-consuming at all) to turn these little activities we are already doing into exercises that quickly, easily, and hopefully enjoyably benefit our health.

In addition to fostering our creativity, it turns out that variety is also good for our health. The best exercise routines actually contain a mix of cardio, flexibility, and strength training. This type of variety keeps our bodies in the proper balance and health. Specifically, flexibility protects us from injury, strength training prevents osteoporosis, and cardio builds our heart health. Variety is truly a key to keeping our exercise beneficial, interesting, and enjoyable.

Putting It into Practice

The point is this: Exercise does not have to be a chore. It can actually be fun. Yes, we may have to overcome some serious misconceptions about the expense, pain, unpleasantness, location, and even time exercise takes. We may have to open our minds in new ways to thinking outside the box, thus overcoming the restrictions we've unconsciously placed on exercise for so long. As we do, we may find that we can actually discover activities and other things we enjoy (e.g., music, nature) to make exercise exciting. Keeping exercise fresh and new by mixing it up will also help with keeping it enjoyable. It's true: It is possible to enjoy, rather than dread, exercise.

As we are able to make this transition to enjoying exercise, we are then able to reap the benefits of exercise—physically, cognitively, and emotionally. Overall, our health improves both now and in the long-term. Even more importantly, we are able to get over the "just do it" mentality so that we can actually maintain an exercise "routine" for the long-haul.

We will acknowledge that this transition from the long-entrenched misconceptions about exercise to something enjoyable can sometimes be slow. Many of us have a lot to overcome in the process. Nonetheless, we believe it is entirely possible because we've both experienced it. So where do you start? Take this chapter's challenge!

Find something that involves a form of physical activity which you think you might enjoy. Ideally, it might be something you've enjoyed in the past, even if you never thought about it as exercise. Be aware that you may have to adapt the activity some way (e.g., turning a love of dancing at weddings into a spontaneous dance party at home). For those who can't find something they've enjoyed in the past, think about things you might enjoy. What have you always thought looked fun but never tried? Also, what can you pair with it (e.g., music, friends, competition) to make it more enjoyable? This is step one: Find some physical activity that you might enjoy.

Keep in mind that this activity does not have to be strenuous, happen in a specific location, or even take up your whole day. If you'd prefer to simply capitalize on the daily trips to the water cooler, see how it feels to take the stairs on the way there at least five times during the day. The important thing is to overcome those misconceptions and get creative. If you get stuck with this, ask a friend for some help thinking outside the box.

Once you've figured out your activity, you're ready for step 2: Try it! Ideally, the activity would take at least 20-30 minutes of your day (even if these minutes aren't all back-to-back). If you can, try to activity at least three days during the week. One important caution with this, however: Don't overdo it. Sometimes we want to go from being a couch potato to a marathon runner overnight, only succeeding in injuring ourselves and becoming miserable in the process. Take it slow and remember to *enjoy* the activity as much as possible. It's not a race or a "to do item"—it's fun! As always, complete the questions for reflection when you are done with your exercise experiment.

Questions for Reflection

1) What did I believe about and expect from exercise, prior to reading this chapter and trying it in a new way this week?

2) What was my actual experience of exercise this week? If I wasn't able to complete it, why not? *(Note: This latter question is a time for gentle curiosity and self-reflection—not self-condemnation; even "failing" to meet our goals is a great source of information that can lead us to success next time.)*

3) Specifically, what was positive about my experience of exercise this week? What did I enjoy?

4) Overall, how did my experience compare to my original beliefs?

5) What's next in my journey of transitioning exercise from being a burden to being a blessing?

Tip #8: Ditch the Diets

Any time we want to lose weight, we have to diet…right? If we or someone around us is overweight, it seems the answer is obvious: Simply cut down on those carbs or other calories and increase the exercise. Dieting is our universal answer to establishing and maintaining a healthy weight.

Unfortunately, this answer is wrong. Diets fail 95-98% of the time. It's true: 95-98% of people on diets either fail to lose weight or gain it all back within a relatively short period of time. We tend to attribute this failure to our will power and other internal factors. Clearly, things like willpower do make a difference. However, if we were talking about a surgery, teaching strategy, or anything else with a 95-98% failure rate, would we really blame the failure on the person receiving the operation or teaching and encourage them to keep using it? Absolutely not. It's time to face the facts: Although we may be doing things to contribute to the failure of our diets, they fail us just as much if not more than we fail them. Diets simply don't work.

Before we move on to talking about what actually does work, some people may be wondering why they haven't heard that diets don't work before. There are probably a lot of reasons, but we'll throw out two. First, the diet industry makes a lot of money. They have absolutely no interest in changing it—after all, most of their customers come back again and again even after their products fail. We can't think of a more ridiculous and yet profitable business model! Second, we are a culture that's afraid of obesity. In our opinion, this fear is much more intense than it needs to be. For now though, let's just say that in our fear, we find it really important to fight obesity and we don't know any ways to do this other than dieting. As an industry and a culture, we stick to diets because they make money by claiming to address a fear that we have—obesity—in a quick-fix way.

Unfortunately, it's time to face the truth that diets aren't working and begin looking for another way—no matter how uncomfortable this may make us. In this chapter, we'll combine our experience and expertise to show you in a little more detail why diets don't work and provide an alternative.[3] It's important to note that this information applies to everyone, at any weight, not just those who fight their weight on the dieting roller-coaster. Whether we physically wear every calorie we eat or have an insanely fast metabolism that burns it all up, what we eat matters for our health. Yes, it is possible to be stick-thin and still physically unhealthy because of the foods we eat. As a result, most of us—regardless of our weight—can benefit from taking a closer look at how we approach food. The information in this chapter is in no way exhaustive, yet we hope it will open minds to approaching the dreaded topics of nutrition, food, and weight in a whole new way.

---

[3] Keep in mind that we aren't medical doctors or nutritionists, so it's important to consult with your doctor before actually making any significant changes to your diet.

Diets—More Harm Than Good

As we begin to open our minds, it's important to really understand that our age-old fall back—dieting—doesn't work. There are many reasons for this. First of all, our bodies are physiologically more concerned about survival than our cultural ideal of beauty. For most of the history of humanity, this meant worrying about not getting enough food and starving to death. The result is that our bodies are very apt to store extra calories in the form of surplus pounds in case we need them later. At the same time, our bodies are much less prone to shed extra calories or pounds even when we decrease our food intake because they think we may need the surplus tomorrow or next year when our "storehouses" dry up. It turns out that our personal experiences are actually based in a solid, physiological reality: It's much easier to gain weight than to lose it.[i]

But, some people might say, isn't it as simple as "calories in and calories out"? Not at all. Physiologically, our body often interprets the severe calorie restrictions of diets as starvation and works even harder to hold onto any excess calories and weight. Remember, our bodies want to survive above all—even if this means working against us while we are dieting. Also, as we've been discussing all along, our bodies are holistic. This means that our emotional realities and other factors also play into the equation too. We may be eating or even holding onto excess weight for emotional reasons rather than physical ones. For example, sadness or boredom may drive us to eat and fear may cause us to hold onto those extra pounds. We'll talk a little more about this later. For now, let us just note that diets don't work because of both physiological and emotional factors.

What's more, diets actually end up harming most of us in the long run. Physiologically, some experts say that diets actually drive our weight up over time.[i] We'll spare you all the complicated science, while concurring that most people we know who have been dieting for a long time actually weigh more today than they did at the outset. In addition, diets tend to keep us emotionally trapped in a cycle of elation and shame. When the scale dips down, we feel great. When it tips the other direction, however—as it does for 95-98% of dieters—we feel ashamed, guilty, and more. We feel really bad, and we often end up "hiding" from others (physically or emotionally) because we are convinced there is something wrong with us (rather than our diets). Although we could write a whole book on this topic alone, suffice it to say that diets not only don't work, they actually do us more harm than good—physiologically, emotionally, and relationally.

The Alternative: Mindful Eating

Although diets fail miserably on many levels, there is an alternative. And, no, we aren't talking about eating whatever we want regardless of the consequences to our bodies. Nor are we talking about intense self-discipline through every day of our lives. We are talking about a growing movement referred to as attuned or mindful eating.

Mindful eating encourages us to follow our body's lead in our eating habits. We may start by being mindful as we eat; remember, as we discussed in "Tip #6: Be Still & Know that I Am," mindfulness involves being nonjudgmentally present with what's happening now. For food, this may involve eating slowly and noticing the taste, texture, etc. of our food. The movement referred to as attuned or mindful eating takes this mindfulness one step further, encouraging us to specifically be mindful of the following three things: (1) Eating when we're hungry, (2) Eating what we're actually hungry for, and (3) Stopping when we're full. The principle behind mindful eating is that our bodies know what we need—both in terms of quantity and substance—and they will direct us appropriately if we let them.

Dr. White: "I grew up in an overweight family, where food was a real issue. By the time I graduated from high school, I was obese. I had tried to lose weight a number of times, particularly through unsuccessful attempts at exercise I hated. Not surprisingly, it never worked. My weight sometimes yo-yoed a bit, but it kept going up overall. Then I went to college. I lost 30 pounds my freshman year without even really trying. This 'success' launched me on a five or six year journey of beginning to develop a healthier lifestyle. As we discussed before, this gradually included exercising that I enjoyed. It also included healthier and healthier foods—not to follow a diet or other restrictive plan, but because I had an increasing desire to feel physically good. As I followed this desire, my food choices naturally changed; I found myself eating less and eating healthier foods. And, lo and behold, I kept losing weight! Dieting had failed me miserably, yet following my body's lead to healthier fare and activities naturally led me to lose (and keep off) 100 pounds."

This principle of mindful eating may sound really strange to many people, especially those who have dieted consistently. Dieters tend to divide foods into "good" and "bad." For example, proteins are good and carbs are bad. Or, perhaps veggies are good and sweets are bad. Whatever the division, dieters follow a very predictable pattern: They want what they can't have. In other words, they begin craving the "forbidden" foods—whether that's carbs or cookies—and eventually binge on what they "can't have." As a result, this shift in actually listening to one's body can take awhile; it takes time to erase the arbitrary "good" versus "bad" distinction and actually tune into what our bodies physically want and need. So, yes, we acknowledge mindful eating is a big and often slow switch for a lot of people.

Having said that, we stand by the fact that mindful eating works. In fact, research is beginning to show that mindful eating is even more effective than dieting. Specifically, one study showed that women in a mindful eating group completed the program with better physical health, higher self-esteem, and an improved relationship with food; the women in the comparable dieting group had only a little weight loss to show for their time and effort…all of which they quickly regained.[i] People who replace dieting with mindful eating tend to end up at a stable weight with greater health, a better relationship with their body, and an increased enjoyment of food.[4] Mindful eating is clearly a paradigm shift that works.

The Challenge: Internal vs. External Choices

The challenge and the beauty of mindful eating is that it switches the basis of our food choices from external to internal. Most people (particularly Americans) tend to eat based off external cues and circumstances. For example, we fill our plate and eat all the food on it—regardless of how hungry or full we feel. We also indulge because the TV's on…or because our co-workers are partaking of donuts at the business meeting—again, without any real thought to whether we even want the donut. Even diets are a form of external rules or cues that tell us what to eat and what not to eat. Typically, we eat according to external cues and circumstances.

Mindful eating turns all of this on its head, asking us to listen to and follow internal cues. It involves learning to tune into our bodies and make assessments about things like hunger and fullness. It also involves learning to distinguish between a variety of signals we

[4] Please note that Dr. White's results of losing and keeping off 100 pounds may not be typical. Actual weight loss is impacted by many factors, including age, genetics, history, and more. Nonetheless, most people who engage in mindful eating are able to find and maintain a much healthier weight than they do under the yo-yo of dieting!

may hear from our bodies. For example, is that grumbling in our stomach a result of physical hunger, boredom, or indigestion? Is our "craving" for that ice cream related to our physical needs/hunger, or a direct result of having a really hard day? Mindful eating invites us to tune into our internal cues and demands that we become good at distinguishing between the sensations we discover.

The ability to make these distinctions is very tricky for a lot of people. It requires a lot of skills, including emotional intelligence. We have to be able to identify our feelings and then respond to them appropriately. Again, for example, if we're craving ice cream because we've had a tough day, we have to be able to identify our frustration or sadness about the day and then respond to it appropriately. Responding "appropriately" may actually involve talking to a friend about our feelings or going for a walk to blow off some steam. Eating ice cream is probably a quicker but much less efficient fix, as it usually just helps us stuff our feelings. Hence, it turns out that mindful eating actually requires a lot of emotional intelligence in addition to physical attunement.

It's outside of the scope of this chapter to fully discuss all of the things that lead us to eat or the skills we need to cope with them effectively. Suffice it to say that mindful eating is a journey that goes way beyond the number on a scale. It's an invitation to look inside of ourselves—at the internal cues and signals—rather than just outside. As a result, mindful eating ends up being much more holistic than the ways we typically approach food or our bodies. This aspect can make it both scary and amazing. The holistic nature of mindful eating is also what makes it work, unlike traditional diet programs.

The Benefit: Health for Life

Because mindful eating is so holistic, the benefits of it extend well beyond the number on a scale as well. As we mentioned earlier, many people do lose weight as a result of sustained, mindful eating. Most everyone establishes a stable weight that they can feel happy about. What's more, people's health usually improves, resulting in things like lowered blood pressure and cholesterol. In addition, those who practice mindful eating tend to feel better about themselves and enjoy both their bodies and food more. It's true—the benefits of mindful eating extend diversely to the physiological and emotional realms.

One benefit we'd particularly like to highlight is the increasing desire and ability to simply feel good physically. As Dr. White's story illustrated, this desire often leads to healthier and healthier food choices. As we are mindful of how things feel in our body—both when we eat them and afterward—it's very common to naturally gravitate toward foods that give us more energy, greater focus, and better digestion. Not surprisingly, these tend to be more natural, healthy foods—yes, if we pay attention, fruits and veggies usually do feel better in our bodies that fried foods! Mindful eating simply leads to healthier eating—not because of some diets rules, but out of an internal desire to feel good.

Dr. Puff: "As I mentioned earlier in the book, I grew up in a family where French fries were considered vegetables. I've come a long way since then. Actually, I've found that I now choose to eat 'raw' for the majority of the day. 'Raw' eating involves sticking to uncooked fruits and vegetables as well as other natural foods, like nuts. I don't tell myself I have to eat these things—I simply enjoy them. It's true! Even if someone could give me rich, heavy, or greasy foods that were calorie-free, I'd turn them down because I prefer the taste and experience of healthier foods. I may have initially chosen to gravitate toward healthier foods because they felt better in my body after I ate them; now, however, I really just enjoy them more. For me, healthy eating is a matter of preference on many levels rather than the painful self-discipline people often construe it as."

As Dr. Puff's story illustrates, eating mindfully doesn't involve a lot of "should's" and other rules. It involves a lot of desire for healthier things. Lest this sound absolutely crazy, allow us to note that our tastebuds do adjust over time to what we're eating.[xix] As a result, it is entirely possible to come to a place where we choose healthy foods both because they feel good in our bodies *and* because we actually prefer the taste over unhealthier foods. This may not be a quick shift or fix, but it allows us to stick to healthy choices for a lifetime…and enjoy them in the process.

Putting It into Practice

In case anyone missed it the first five times, we'll say it again: Diets don't work. They literally fail 95-98% of the time. They fail for many reasons—both physiological and emotional. From our viewpoint, the biggest problem is that diets aren't holistic enough. They continue to encourage us on a path of overly-simplistic thinking (e.g., "calories in, calories out") and an external focus (i.e., "good" vs. "bad" foods). It's truly time to ditch the diets.

So where does that leave us? Although it can be a difficult and often slow shift to make, we advocate for eating mindfully based on internal cues of hunger and fullness. This method tends to be much more effective at helping to control our weight in a lasting way. What's more, making this switch also leads to a variety of physiological and emotional benefits beyond the number of a scale, including the desire and enjoyment of simply being healthy. Mindful eating is a new, challenging paradigm we invite you to consider.

In fact, we'd like to challenge you to try a little mindful eating experiment right now. For this experiment, you'll need to choose an upcoming meal that you can eat alone in a quiet place. You'll need to eat sitting down, preferably at a kitchen table or someplace else specifically designed for meals. It's also critical that you remove all distractions—that's right, no TV, cell phones, or other electronic devices. Preferably, this experiment would even be done without other people around or even any music. The first step for this experiment, in other words, is to find a quiet place where you can have an undistracted meal.

Once you've carved out the space and time, prepare your meal and enjoy! We'll only give you two catches: First, set a timer and try to make your meal last at least 20-30 minutes (yes, this may sound like a long time in our fast-paced, eat-on-the-go society, so feel free to pace yourself). Second, pay attention *internally* while you are eating. Before you even begin, do you feel hungry? How does this hunger change as you continue to eat? Are there other feelings or sensations that come up? If so, how do they impact your desire to eat? What leads you to stop eating (e.g., the end of your time, finishing all your food, an internal feeling of fullness)? In short, the second step for this experiment is to eat mindfully.

As with many of our experiments, it's critical to conduct oneself with benign curiosity and graciousness. Some people may discover they are eating "comfort food" because of boredom rather than hunger. It may be tempting to become self-critical with this information. We encourage you not to take this path. No matter what you discover, this is new information that can be used later to establish healthier and more mindful eating. Simply think of yourself like an explorer noticing and cataloguing a new world—without judgment! As usual, complete the questions for reflection below when you are finished.

Questions for Reflection

1) What did I initially think about this experiment? In other words, what thoughts or feeling arise as I think of spending time with only myself and food?

2) What was the easiest and best thing about this experiment?

3) What was the hardest thing (e.g., being alone, the length of time)?

4) What did I notice *internally* as I ate mindfully? Does this information teach me anything about myself and my typical relationship with food?

5) *Bonus Question:* How did the food feel in my body 30-60 minutes after my meal (e.g., heavy, satisfying)? (In other words, you get to continue your mindfulness even as you complete these questions.)

Note: For further information and practice with eating mindfully, sign up for Dr. White's free informational videos at www.dietfreeforever.co.

Tip #9: Know Thy Limits

In this chapter, we'd like to add to the age-old wisdom of the Ten Commandments. Our goal is not to be sacrilegious, but to playfully acknowledge that we may need additional help meeting the unique demands of the 21st century. So here is a new commandment which is very much needed, yet often overlooked today: *Know thy limits.* Perhaps we could even state, know *and respect* thy limits.

We've acknowledged many times throughout this book that we live in a fast-paced world. It will truly take all we can give it and much more. How do we deal with this? Most of us give and give…ending up exhausted and haggard—without, ironically, ever feeling that we have actually given enough. The little bits of time we get to rest or recuperate never satisfy. Unfortunately, though, we just continue to ignore these real needs or desires for rest, living instead according to the busyness and task lists ahead of us.

Sadly, this haggardness takes a toll on us in every way. Our bodies are exhausted. It's harder to concentrate and even muster up excitement for things we used to enjoy. We are more prone to anxiety, depression, and simply emotional melt-downs. We're also more impatient and possibly even distant or conflicted in our relationships. And God? Well, even if He's important to us, He probably seems a million miles away because we can't find the time or energy to connect with Him well either. It's true—our exhaustion takes a toll on us physically, emotionally, relationally, and even spiritually.

If we truly want to experience the happiness and success of a holistic life, we must reverse this trend. We must learn to own our agendas, respecting our limits as much as the task lists or other busyness. On a day-to-day basis this could probably refer to a lot of things. In this chapter, we'll start with the basics, like reducing stress and getting enough sleep. Sound familiar? Absolutely. *But do we do it?* If so, you have our complete permission to skip ahead. If not, however, it may be important to read on, remembering why these basics are important and beginning to figure out how to actually integrate them into our lives.

Stress: Innocent or Injurious?

As if we haven't hit upon enough disturbing words in this section (e.g., exercise, nutrition), here's another one: STRESS. It may be stressful simply to see it there in all caps! Stress is something we're very familiar with. It can come from good things, like getting married, and from difficult things, like losing a job. It can also be related to huge occurrences, like the death of a loved one, or minor incidences, like the daily traffic jam. Stress is a part of our lives—one that seems to be dreaded yet simply endured. So what's the truth about stress?

First of all, stress is a normal part of life that doesn't have to be bad. We all know what it feels like to experience stress; as long as we are a part of the human race, we are unlikely to get away from it. Good news though—this isn't necessarily bad. Small amounts of stress can physiologically provide us the energy and motivation we need to complete important tasks (e.g., finish that project at work or school, prepare for that upcoming change in our life). Some stress is actually good.

Stress becomes an issue, however, when it's constant. When stress is present on an ongoing, overwhelming basis in our lives, then it starts to cause problems. More specifically, chronic stress can diminish our brain functioning by reducing blood flow. It can also lead to all kinds of emotional problems, like depression and anxiety. Chronic stress also weakens our immune system, resulting in health problems ranging from the common cold to a heart attack. What's more, chronic stress can even make us look worse by aging us prematurely and indirectly leading to weight gain.[xx] Clearly, chronic stress is a problem for us—physiologically, neurologically, and even emotionally.

Stress, then, can be either innocent or injurious, helpful or harmful, depending on its frequency and intensity in our lives. This is good news and bad. The good news is that we don't need to beat ourselves up for experiencing stress or try to get rid of it all together. The bad news is that stress can hurt or even kill us if it gets out-of-control. Consequently, our goal should be to keep the levels of stress in our lives under control, so it remains helpful to us instead of hurtful.

5 Tips for Stress Management

So how do we keep our levels of stress under control? Consider these suggestions:

1) Cut Out the Excess: A huge contributor to stress is simply having too much to do. We're bound to feel keyed up and stressed out when we're exhausted from trying to "do it all." As a result, the first, and perhaps most difficult, stress-reduction technique is simply to evaluate what we are doing and cut out the excess. What is really, truly necessary? What do we actually enjoy and feel invigorated by? How can we delegate or simplify things that don't fit these categories? One difficult thing about this step is defining what's really important and necessary to us versus what's important to our friends or family. It's time to live our lives and let them live theirs—even if this means not keeping pace with some of the things they value more than us.

2) Enjoy the Journey: Once we cut out the excess, the next step is to try and enjoy what's actually left on our plate. This may be a whole lot easier when our plate is simply less crowded. We can also do a lot to increase our enjoyment by adjusting our environment, schedule, and more. For example, perhaps working at our desk would be more enjoyable if we put up some pictures or played some soft music we enjoyed. Maybe we'd also be invigorated by taking some short breaks to meditate or call a friend instead of working every moment of the day. In addition, we might enjoy lunch if we went for a walk, read a book, or planned time with some friends or co-workers we like. There are many little things we can do to make our environment a more pleasant place and our schedule a more livable frame.

Dr. Puff: "Since I spend most of the day at my office, I intentionally make it a place I enjoy. For example, I light candles and turn on soft music to make it a meditative place, which fits my personality. Years ago, I also started bringing Einstein to work with me. My clients enjoy having a dog around, but I confess that it's really me who gets the most benefit. I'm also careful to schedule and take breaks, during which I usually walk around and get some fresh air, in order to keep up my energy during the day. Actually, my whole environment and day are built around the principle of self-care. I figure out what I need first, and then I allot work into the time that's left over. Most people do it in reserve (i.e., work, then rest with the time left over), but I've found that putting self-care first makes me a better, happier, and more effective person in every area of my life. When I put this philosophy together with all of the little things I do in my environment, I'm able to enjoy my day rather than come home stressed out and worn down."

3) Control the Mind: Once we've simplified our schedule a bit and made our environment more positive, we are in a better place to actually enjoy our day. How do we accomplish this? First, we practice the sense of awareness and presence that we discussed earlier in the book. We also try to focus on the positive and let go of the negative. This may sometimes involve letting go of frustrating or difficult situations (e.g., the unexpected traffic jam we hit this morning, the extra report our child needs our help finishing today); at these times, it may be helpful to take a minute to vent…and then move on. It's easy to ruin our day and the moods of those around us by dwelling on and rehashing the frustrations in our day again and again. Although the frustrations are understandable, we help ourselves more by remembering the impermanence of these stressors and moving on to more present, positive things.

4) Plan Stress Reduction Activities: Hopefully our stress will be reduced through steps 1-3 above…and yet there are still times it will get the best of us. This is why it's important to plan stress reduction activities on a regular basis. As we noted earlier, taking breaks throughout our day may be relieving. Daily meditation and exercise are also great techniques for reducing stress. Weekly time to be creative, playful, or simply with friends may also be helpful. In addition, we advocate regular retreats and vacations to simply take a break from it all. It's important to plan these things on a consistent basis as well as leaving some space to just do them spontaneously. Although the specific activity isn't necessarily important, leaving space in our lives for stress reduction is critical.

5) Reward Yourself: Last but not least, it's also important to celebrate our milestones and reward our successes. We are much more able to handle a particularly busy day or season without falling into chronic stress if we take the time to de-compress regularly. This may mean taking breaks. It may involve doing "something nice" for ourselves. Whatever it looks like, it's a good idea to reward ourselves with healthy things we enjoy on a daily or even weekly basis. How much easier would it be to face the busyness of tomorrow if we had the opportunity to read a book, take a bath, go for a run, or whatever else we enjoy for even 20 or 30 minutes tonight? And don't worry—celebrating what we've accomplished and rewarding our own hard work won't spoil us; it'll simply make us more ready to face tomorrow with less stress.

Dr. White: "I recently finished a huge milestone in my career—my psychology license. The completion of this milestone marked the culmination of an eight-year journey, starting from the time I applied for graduate school. In spite of my self-care during my degree, I felt exhausted as soon as I finished the last hurdle on this path. Although there were many doors that opened to me once finishing, I decided to put them on hold for a month and simply use any excess time in my schedule for resting and celebrating. I knew those other doors would still be there in a month, and I'd probably be much more invigorated to open them after a break. For the month, it was time to simply celebrate and reward myself for a job well done."

One More Tip on Stress Management…Sleep!

The last tip for stress management is so important that it deserves a section of it's own. This tip is also the most basic: Get good rest. We seem to treat sleep as a "nice to have" item in our culture. We like to get a good amount of it, but we don't really structure our schedules in a way to make sure this happens consistently. As a result, many of us run on empty simply because we are physiologically depleted from a lack of sleep.

Fortunately or unfortunately, it turns out that sleep is a critical factor for our health. Research shows that sleep deprivation is associated with a number of negative factors, such as weight gain, premature aging and other skin problems, poor concentration and planning, difficulty with problem-solving, decreased coordination and other difficulties with motor functioning. Sleep deprivation also makes us grumpier and more irritable, which is not super helpful for our family or social life. In addition, it puts us at greater risk for a number of health conditions, such as depression, diabetes, anxiety, ADHD, Alzheimer's, Parkinson's, stroke, and even psychosis.[xx] Truly, sleep is *critical* for our physical and emotional well-being.

So how much is enough? The amount can vary somewhat by age, physiology, physical practices, etc. A great place for adults to start is 7-8 hours of sleep per night…yes, *every* night! From there, we can be mindful of whether we need even more sleep. Children and adolescents definitely need more. For many of us, achieving 7+ hours of sleep is simply a matter of adjusting our schedule to have enough space in our day for sleep. We'll refer those people back to step one above—cutting out the excess. Others of us seem to have difficulty falling and staying asleep in spite of our best intentions. For these people, consider these tips:

~Practice good health during the day: The way we spend the 16 or so hours between sleep cycles significantly impacts the quality of our sleep. Things like regular exercise and meditation will likely improve our sleep, whereas large amounts of caffeine and other stimulants may harm it.

~Beware of sleep killers: Although it seems obvious, sometimes our sleep can be disturbed by the little things, like drinking caffeine or napping too late in the day. Even eating, exercising, or watching TV late at night can be stimulating in a way that wakes us up rather than winds us down. Drinking alcohol can be a deceptive sleep killer too, as it initially makes us drowsy and then often disrupts sleep cycles. Those who are having trouble sleeping may need to pay attention to these little factors and assess their sleep patterns long before bed.

~Develop a bedtime routine: Instead of drinking caffeine, watching TV, or other things that might wake us up, it can be helpful to do relaxing things before bedtime. For example, we might drink a cup of herbal tea, take a warm bath, or listen to some soft music. Ideally, we'll even consider developing a routine before bed that involves the same relaxing activities every night so that

these activities become stimuli that cue our bodies it's time to wind down.

~Follow a regular sleep schedule: As difficult as it may be, it's important to go to sleep and get up at roughly the same time everyday. Our bodies begin to adjust to these rhythms and engage in them more smoothly.

~Reserve the bed for sleep: When we're having difficulty falling asleep, it is sometimes because bed has become a place for reading, watching TV, or even thinking over the worries of the day. Try to make bed a place only for sleeping (or sexual activity), which may even mean getting up and taking a break if one doesn't fall asleep within 20-30 minutes.

~Deal with outstanding difficulties: Outstanding problems can easily interfere with our sleep. Some of the biggest culprits are mental health problems, like depression and anxiety. For those who know (or suspect) such difficulties may be interfering with their sleep, it's time to visit a mental health practitioner who can help (e.g., a psychologist who can treat the disorder and maybe even a psychiatrist to prescribe meds for the sleep problems in the meantime).

Each of these tips—from establishing a regular routine to dealing with any difficulties interfering with our sleep—will help us to sleep better overall.

Putting It into Practice

Some of the biggest joy-stealers and health-killers in our lives are the simplest: Stress and exhaustion. Although small amounts of stress can actually be helpful and one night of poor sleep probably won't kill us, large amounts of chronic stress or sleep deprivation can really do a lot of harm. We tend to have a "yeah, yeah" sort of attitude that doesn't really take these factors seriously. Research shows us, however, that they have the potential to harm us in every area—body, heart, relationships, and more. It's time to really stop and begin to value our health and happiness enough that we take our stress and sleep seriously.

As we finally begin to take our stress and sleep seriously, we have to recognize and respect our limits. Like it or not, we are human *beings*—not human *doings*—so we cannot run ourselves into the ground like machines. We need rest, play, and all kinds of self-care to run properly. And (spoiler alert!), no one else will do this for us. We must each take responsibility for our own health and lives, even if it means making some tough decisions regarding our agendas. The best place to start with these decisions is cutting out the excess, enjoying the journey, controlling our minds, planning stress reduction activities, rewarding ourselves for a job well-done, and even getting enough sleep. These are the ways that we know and respect our limits.

Ready to get started? We'd like to challenge you to start knowing and respecting your limits for just one week. Here's how you do it: First, sit down and write out your schedule for the entire week. This may take a little time because it should include everything from the hours you spend at work to the 15 minutes you spend running by the dry cleaner. When you're done, look over your schedule. What immediately sticks out as excess that might be simplified or delegated? For example, can you carpool the kids to school this week instead of taking them yourself everyday? Mark these things right away and begin making the adjustments to cut them down or out for the week.

Here's where it really gets tricky. Your challenge is to pare down your schedule enough that you can get at least 7-8 hours of sleep *every night* and spend at least 30-60 minutes *every day* in some sort of stress reduction activity (i.e., healthy things you enjoy that de-stress you). Ideally, you'd also make space for some extended time of rest and play sometime during the week, like a ½ day or full day over the weekend. You may have to get really creative and possibly even ask others for help in order to clear your schedule enough to make this possible. Just remember though—for now, it's only one week; there's no reason that some of the things on your calendar can't be put off or delegated for at least that long.

Once you've cleared the space, plan and calendar your sleep and stress reduction activities (in pen!) so that they are set in stone for the week. This will be your sacred, unbendable time during the week as much as you can make that happen. Like all of our challenges, however, it's important to be gracious with yourself when things don't go exactly as you planned; even the inability to meet our goals can be great information for future growth. Once you've completed the week, return and answer the questions for reflection below.

Questions for Reflection

1) What was the hardest part about this challenge—cutting out the excess, following through with stress reduction activities, sleeping, or something else?

2) What was the best and most rewarding part of this challenge?

3) How did it feel to simply acknowledge my limits and focus more on my own self-care this week?

4) What did I learn about myself? Specifically, do I have a need for greater stress management, and/or any specific challenges to address in following through with it?

5) How can I practice knowing and respecting my limits in future weeks by applying what I've learned? Do I need help from anyone around me in order to make this happen?

Tying It All Together

The three most important components of keeping our bodies healthy are: (1) the amount of physical activity we engage in, (2) how we eat, and (3) our stress level. The bad news, for many of us, is that these things really do matter and add up to impact our overall health and success in the long-run. The good news is that they don't have to make us miserable. Exercise, for example, can actually be fun if we can get past the serious misconceptions we carry about it, and think outside the box a little. Pretty soon, we can reap the physical, cognitive, and emotional benefits of moving our bodies as we shift our attitude of "just do it" to one of *"just enjoy it."*

At the same time, we have to shift our diet mentalities. Diets fail over and over again because they are too simplistic and don't take the whole person into account. This doesn't mean we have to just stay where we're at though. In fact, as we make a shift from living by external cues, like diet rules, to focusing on the internal cues of our hunger and fullness, we can actually enjoy our food more and control our weight in a lasting way. It is possible to *ditch the diets* and actually find new freedom, life, and success in this area.

The third, most critical, piece of finding physical success is watching our stress levels. Although a little stress is okay, large amounts of chronic stress really will harm us—physically, emotionally, interpersonally, and more. As we learn to take our stress seriously, we learn the importance of respecting our limits, whether they move us toward sleeping, cutting out excess, planning for self-care, or some other activity. Like it or not, we are human beings—not human doings—and we function better when we *know and respect thy limits.*

These are the three most important components to thriving physically: being active, eating a healthy diet, and controlling our levels of stress. If we can accomplish these things, we'll do pretty well in terms of weight, blood pressure, heart health, and more. Sounds simple? Yes, but we recognize these three "simple" things are often pretty hard for people in practice. As a result, we tend to fall into extremes of either ignoring these areas or trying to be well-oiled machines. We think it's important to instead establish a middle ground—a place where we can find health by combining the discipline of a professional dancer with activities that the child spontaneously does and enjoys.

Part IV: Heart

What makes dancing rich and beautiful? Is it the skill of the dancers? Yes. But is that all? Imagine the performance of a dancer who can execute perfect skill, yet she does not care about or enjoy the art at all. Regardless of her skill, she would lack a certain fluidity and beauty that comes with the love and passion of her art. She would likely come off as rather stale and flat. This is because our heart adds a richness and beauty to life.

In this area, the spontaneity of the child may sometimes trump the skill of the master. After all, it's the heart of the child that makes her dance delightful to watch. It's her passion and abandon—not skill—that make it a joy to witness the child dancing. It's the fact that she is putting her whole heart and soul into the moment, embracing and enjoying it fully, that makes the child's dance seem delightful. Truly, the addition of true passion and heart into any dance, at any age, is a key component to making it beautiful.

Whether we are aware of it or not, the same is true of our dance through life. Our heart matters. It adds the richness, color, and texture to life. This is where we get the beauty and depth to our lives. It's where we find a sense of meaning, purpose, and significance too. Yes, even for the most logical amongst us, our hearts matter.

Allow us one point of clarification: Like that skilled dancer with no passion, we can function pretty well for long stretches of time without heart. We can execute the right steps and perhaps even stay in time with the music. However, we are unlikely to enjoy the dance or really look beautiful to others. At some point, we may also run into a particularly emotionally-laden piece of music—or part of life, like the death of a loved one—and simply be unable to move through it because of the heart it requires. In other words, not connecting to our hearts won't necessarily sabotage us on day one; instead, it will more likely whittle us (or our relationships) away over time, leaving life rather flat overall, and perhaps even making us quite stuck when emotional dilemmas arise.

As a result, it behooves us to live with heart now. This allows us to navigate successfully through all of life. It also adds a beauty and richness to the day-to-day. How do we do it? Well, emotional health requires that we can effectively utilize the messages, cues, and experience of our emotions...without being overwhelmed by them. In other words, we want to tap into their beauty and richness without turning life into some crazy, abstract painting. At the same time, it's also important to tap into the depth of our spirituality. These key components will allow us to fully utilize our hearts, embracing some of the abandon and passion of the care-free child.

Tip #10: Mind the Messenger

The physical body is an amazing thing. It has the ability to walk and run and jump, and it even tells us when it needs something. For example, our eyes and limbs feels heavy when we need sleep. Our stomach grumbles when our body needs fuel. What's more, our finger hurts when it is touching a hot surface and needs to be moved. The body gives us all kind of cues related to its internal workings and needs.

Imagine for a moment that we ignored these cues. Perhaps we felt the grumblings in our stomach or pain in our finger and did nothing. Maybe we were even so out of touch with our bodies' cues that we actually missed these signals that the body needed something. What would happen then? First, we'd likely feel some new physical symptoms, like sluggishness, difficulty concentrating, and more pain. If we continued to ignore these cues as well, we'd eventually find ourselves in trouble—with a bad burn or eventually even malnourishment. Although some are more urgent than others, the body's cues are messages that we need to heed.

Few people would disagree that the body provides critical messages for us to follow, but a lot would argue the same point related to emotions. When it comes to our emotions, many people think it is okay to tune them out...unless, perhaps, they are convenient or feel good. Unfortunately, this just isn't true. Like physical cues, our emotions are messengers that cue us when something is happening or needed. Ignoring our emotional cues can be just as detrimental to our health as ignoring the physical ones. In this chapter, we'll clarify how emotions act as messengers (and more), clear up some misconceptions regarding the importance of emotions, and begin to discuss how to use them.

Emotions: Messengers and Motivators

To start with, what are emotions, and why do we have them? These are very critical questions for us to answer. For some people, emotions seem like the annoying neighbor next door who they can't quite get rid of. For others, emotions feel like the overwhelming family member who invades our space and steals our energy. Although we understand these experiences, we contend that emotions are actually supposed to be the helpful assistant who keeps us on-track. Why? Because they act as both messengers and motivators.

As we touched upon briefly above, emotions are first *messengers* to us. They tell us that something significant is happening; they also provide us an initial assessment for whether it's good or bad, helpful or threatening. For example, most people tend to feel angry and sad when they hear about child abuse. Although this is an extreme example, it illustrates the point well. We feel angry because an injustice has occurred and sad at the loss of innocence for the child. In this way, emotions provide vital messages to us about what's happening in the world around us.

As we all know and have experienced, however, our emotions do not always seem congruent with the circumstances we're encountering. For instance, one might burst out crying because of a small slight, or get serious road rage when someone accidentally cuts him off on the freeway. What is happening here? In these instances, our emotions are providing us messages about what is happening inside of us as well as outside. Our crying outburst may indicate that the small slight hit upon a tender spot or wound that is unresolved in our hearts. Alternatively, the rage we feel when we're cut off may communicate that we're tired or perhaps even upset about something that happened earlier in the day. Hence, our emotions provide us messages about what's happening inside of us as well as outside.

Our emotions also act as *motivators* that move us toward action. Emotions come with a vast amount of energy. As a result, they provide the resources and drive to respond appropriately to ourselves and our environment. For example, most of us would respond to the message about child abuse by protecting and helping the child. This action flows from the emotional energy we feel when we receive the message. On a smaller scale, we might respond to the internal messages we mentioned by getting more rest or resolving the unrelated situation that stirred up the emotion. Some people are so uncomfortable with their emotions that they manage to impede this flow of this energy; this really is to their detriment, however, because the energy is there to *help us* respond appropriately to ourselves and others.

Dr. Puff: "In my early 20's, I began to notice that I would sometimes feel overwhelmed and anxious during the day. When I stopped to assess this feeling, I realized the message was that I had taken on too much. My emotions were telling me that I was over-committed. They were also providing the motivation and energy for me to cut down. No, this wasn't an easy process, but I listened to my emotions and was slowly able to sort through my activities and do less. I'm incredibly thankful for this today, as I'm able to truly enjoy the activities that are actually on my plate since I no longer allow myself to get overcommitted."

As Dr. Puff's story illustrates, our emotions act as messengers and motivators. As messengers, they provide us information about both ourselves and our environment. In this way, they act as teachers, helping us to understand and assess things in a deeper way. At the same time, as motivators, emotions provide the energy for us to take action when needed. Consequently, the important questions to ask ourselves when we feel something are as follows: First, what is this emotion telling me about myself and/or the world around me? Second, what is the appropriate way to respond to this message? In this way, we can capitalize on the messages and motivation provided by our emotions.

5 Common Misconceptions

In order to fully capitalize on the benefits our emotions provide, we need to uncover some common misconceptions that often get us off-track. These misconceptions tend to cause us to either over or underemphasize our emotions, thus preventing us from utilizing our emotions in a truly adaptive way. We'll talk more about how to handle these circumstances a little later in this chapter and the next; for now, allow us to simply begin unpacking a few of the common misconceptions:

1) Emotions don't matter: People who tend to underemphasize their emotions often contend that emotions are unimportant. These people may emphasize the importance of intellect or reason, arguing that emotions are just arbitrary reactions which should be ignored. While we also value intellect and reason, we believe that emotions are incredibly important. As we've discussed above, emotions are an amazing source of information and energy for us. Not using them is first and foremost overlooking an incredible resource we have at our disposable—a resource, remember, which tends to add a lot of color and richness to life too. Ignoring emotions misses these benefits. Because we are impeding the flow of emotional energy through us, ignoring our emotions also tends to back up a lot of energy in our bodies. This unprocessed energy may manifest in a variety of mental and physical difficulties, ranging from digestion problems and physical pain to depression and anxiety. Hence, without meaning to offend those who disagree, we conclude that believing emotions are unimportant and ignoring them is both stupid and dangerous.

2) Emotions are facts: At the other extreme, people who overemphasize emotions often treat them as if they are facts. For these people, feeling sad or angry is equivalent to being wronged or experiencing some injustice. In response to this, remember that emotions communicate about what is happening outside *and inside* of us. Sometimes our emotions tell us as much or more about ourselves as they do about our environment. For example, imagine someone getting reamed by his boss and then going home and over-reacting to a comment of his spouse. Someone who over-emphasizes his emotions might interpret his anger as meaning that his spouse wronged him; in actual fact, the anger would be communicating more about the person's upset over the interactions with his boss. In other words, the anger would be sending a message about an internal state (e.g., ongoing upset about a previous incident) rather than an external one (i.e., the comment the spouse made). Hence, our emotions are critical sources of information that require discernment in understanding and using them appropriately.

3) I'll just feel the good ones: Emotions can be difficult to deal with, especially if we've never been provided skills and training in how to address them. As a result, some people decide (usually unconsciously) that they will just feel the "good" emotions, like happiness and joy, and ignore the "bad" emotions, like anger and sadness. Although we can understand this desire, we've got bad news: It doesn't work. When we cut off one or more emotions, they tend to build up as unprocessed emotional energy and create physical and emotional problems in the long run, as we discussed earlier. What's more, trying to cut off one or more emotions tends to mute and eventually decrease our other emotions as well. In other words, trying to avoid sadness well damper our happiness over time too. Like it or not, our emotions come as a package deal. If we want the information and color they provide for life, we have to learn how to manage the whole gamut.

4) Pain is bad: Implicit in misconception #3 is the additional idea that some emotions, especially pain, are "bad." Sometimes anger, fear, and sadness are added to the "bad" list as well. We'll admit that these emotions can be quite uncomfortable, particularly if we don't know how to mange them. There is good news though: Pain can actually be a helpful messenger and teacher. Like the finger pain which leads us to avoid a burn or the anger which causes us to stop abuse, painful sensations and emotions can tell us important things about both ourselves and the world. In actuality, they can protect and grow us in amazing ways. The key, again, is knowing how to manage the pain or other difficult emotions so that they aren't overwhelming.

5) I'm "too sensitive": This misconception tends to manifest differently for men and women. For men, there is the cultural idea that "real men don't cry," meaning that any emotions (particularly sadness) can feel like too much. For women, there is a cultural idea of being "strong" against difficulty, which sometimes means that women think they should not react to "little things." The reality for both genders, however, is that *healthy people feel.* Period. Our sensitivities may vary based on our personalities and even our season in life, but emotions themselves are universal. We can go wrong if we get carried away by our feelings, engaging in crazy self-talk or treating them as facts, but feeling emotions themselves is simply a part of being human.

If we could summarize the truth about emotions, we'd say this: *Emotions are normal and even good.* Yes, it is possible to overemphasize them or even reach faulty conclusions about what they mean if we aren't discerning. We'll talk more about how to address this extreme in the next chapter. For now, we'd like to address the extreme of underemphasizing one's emotions. These are the people who cut off and miss the amazing gift of their emotions. This type of downplaying of emotions is very common, particularly among certain subsets of the population, like men. Whether male or female, however, if this describes you, we'd like to invite you into the amazing journey of experiencing and utilizing your emotions in a balanced way. This journey truly adds both an amazing resource and richness to life.

Where to Start

So how do we tap into the resource and richness of our emotions in a balanced way? Although it's beyond the scope of this chapter to fully explain this idea, we'd like to give a few starting tips here.

~Open up some space: It's important to give some time to the process, especially for those who are used to simply tuning out or turning off their emotions. For these

people, the first step is to intentionally create some time and space to simply be with one's self. Just as we'd set aside time to get to know a new friend, we need time to get to know the emotional side of ourselves.

~Plan the environment wisely: Logistically, there are some important factors to keep in mind during this time. First, it can be alone or with another person who is capable of helping us connect to our emotions; sometimes this other person can be a friend or family member, but therapists and other professionals can also come in quite handy here. Either way, the time can start small—even five or ten minutes at first, sitting with a cup of tea, a candle, some art, or perhaps some soft music. Although we recommend sitting quietly during this time, some people do find that a long commute home in the car can be a useful place for this experience as long as the radio is turned down or off. The important thing is to have some quiet time aimed at just providing space for the emotional self.

~Use grounding activities: We recognize that this may sound daunting for people who aren't used to giving their emotions space. These readers may be wondering what they actually *do* during this time. It may be helpful to start with some deep breathing, meditation, prayer, or other grounding activity to help settle and connect to one's self. Journaling or collaging with magazines can also be useful. In addition, we recommend using the body to aid in this process. Consider doing a "scan" of the body from the top of the head to the bottom of the feet. What sensations are present? Try sitting with these

sensations and simply seeing what thoughts or emotions arise. Truly, our bodies can be a great window into our emotions.

Dr. White: "I grew up in a way that tended to dismiss and tune out my emotions, so I had to learn how to connect and use my emotions when I became an adult. I found that having space to connect to myself could be a little daunting at first, and it was helpful for me to do something in this time. My favorite activity for a long time was getting old magazines and simply looking through them to see what words or pictures seemed to connect deeply with me. I'd tear out these words or pictures and eventually paste them into my journal. Sometimes the page would end up as a scattered collage, while other times I could integrate the meaningful magazine clippings in with my own thoughts. Either way, I found this activity was a great way for me to safely connect to the emotional parts of myself that sometimes seemed to be in hiding. I almost always felt better afterward—often somewhat "cleansed"—and I was able to act upon the rich messages I was receiving in a more appropriate way."

~Embrace purpose instead of judgment: Once our emotions begin to arise, it's important just to be present with them in a non-judgmental way. Remember, all emotions have a purpose, providing us with messages and motivation to respond to our world and circumstances.

For example, happiness is a message that things are going particularly well. Anger, in contrast, is a message that we perceive some attack or injustice. Sadness is a message that we are experiencing some kind of pain or loss, and fear is a message that we perceive some danger. Regardless of how "good" or "bad" the emotion feels, it can be helpful. Try to look for the message and purpose before judging the feeling or even deciding how to respond to it.

~Be flexible and patient: People may have different experiences of this kind of time. For some, they will be so unaccustomed to connecting with their emotions that it will feel like completely empty space. Others may recognize some vague sensations or feelings that they can't quite pinpoint or name. This will change with time and experience, but it is a normal place to start. In fact, we've sometimes thought of emotions like animals or children; when they become scared, they go into hiding, and they won't come back out until they are certain it's safe. As a result, the important thing is to simply start by being present with ourselves and allow some space for our emotions to come out of hiding. The other skills, including recognizing the specific feeling, message, and appropriate response, will come with time.

It's also important to note that some people may begin to feel new emotions or familiar ones more intensely as they enter into this space. This is normal too. It's also most likely very safe, in spite of how scary the growing intensity of emotions can feel when we aren't used to them. If the intensity becomes too much, it's alright to step away and do something distracting or redirecting (e.g., going for a walk, calling a friend) to find a renewed place of calm. The important thing is simply to not give up on this new friend; take time to get to know these emotions intentionally—regardless of what form or time it takes.

Putting It into Practice

In spite of potentially difficult past experiences, our emotions are meant to be good and helpful. Like it or not, they are also a normal part of life which we avoid at our own peril. Specifically, ignoring our emotions is likely to take some of the luster out of life; it may also create other emotional or physical difficulties over time. Hence, just as we pay attention to our physical cues, trusting them to provide helpful and accurate information, it's time we mind the message within our emotional cues as well.

We'll find it easier to mind the messenger when we get down to the truth about emotions. Emotions aren't at the extreme of facts or fiction; instead, they are somewhere in the middle—a useful source of information that requires discernment. Why? Because emotions provide messages about things happening both outside and inside of us, leaving a lot to sort through. Yes, this "sorting through" can be difficult when we encounter pain or other uncomfortable emotions. However, by building the skills over time, even pain can become a gift and teacher. And it really is much better than the alternative of missing out on the good emotions too. Emotions are truly meant to be our friends.

We've already provided a number of tips for beginning to get to know this friend. It's important to create some space, leave the judgment at the door, use grounding activities and other resources to help connect to ourselves, and then just see what comes up. Over time, we can use these steps to build the skills of connecting to our emotions, naming them, recognizing the messages about ourselves and our world, and responding to them appropriately. Our emotions may then be a welcome friend indeed!

Today, we'd like to invite you to take a step forward in this process. Find a quiet space as we discussed above and then journal for at least five minutes. Do not stop. Do not screen your words. Simply write. (Although typing is acceptable, writing sometimes helps tap into deeper parts of the self.) You don't even have to use complete sentences—just allow yourself to pour out whatever comes to mind. You can stop when five minutes have passed, although going longer is great if there are still words flowing out of you.

When you've finished journaling, take a few deep breaths. Then read back over what you wrote…SLOWLY! If something strikes you, stop and sit with it for awhile. When you've finished reading, take a few minutes to simply sit quietly. What do you notice? Have new thoughts or feelings come up? Are you aware of any sensations in your body? Take your time and then proceed to answer the questions for reflection below.

Questions for Reflection

1) What have my previous experiences been like with emotions (e.g., overwhelming, nonexistent)?

2) Did these previous experiences lead to any misconceptions about emotions that made it difficult for me to enter into this exercise?

3) What emotions arose once I entered in? If I can't name them, how would I describe them to a friend? *(Hint: Feel free to use visual imagery, perhaps starting with any physical sensations you experience.)*

4) Is it possible for me to identify any messages about myself or my life in these emotions or the corresponding thoughts and sensations?

5) Does this message move me to any particular action? If so, how can I carry it out appropriately (i.e., in a

productive way that helps myself and others rather than causing harm)?

Tip #11: Contain the Child

We've all seen a child who throws an enormous tantrum in some public setting. Perhaps we were at the park or a restaurant, and the 2 or 3-year-old near us (or perhaps even with us!) got upset over something seemingly insignificant, like having to go home or share his/her toys. All of a sudden, the fists were flying, the vocal chords were blaring, and we had a full-blown tantrum.

In moments like these, our reaction was probably to look pointedly (and perhaps compassionately) at the parents, hoping they would soon get their child and his/her increasing tantrum under control. If we were the parents or caretakers of the child, we might have also felt a sense of embarrassment, been overwhelmed, and possibly even desired to escape the situation. Whether or not the child was ours, we hoped that his/her emotions would soon be contained—both for the child's sake and our own!

Although we may be less aware of it, our emotions can sometimes feel a lot like this uncontained, tantruming child. Something seemingly insignificant will happen, and our emotions are suddenly flaring or raging, pumping us full of adrenaline, sorrow, or some other intense feeling. This reaction may be completely internal, or it may manifest physically in tears, flailing fists, or other behaviors that can strikingly resemble the tantruming child. At these moments, we are likely either to be carried away by the emotion…or to feel embarrassed, overwhelmed, and like escaping ourselves, wishing only that it would stop.

This emotional experience is common to those who overemphasize, or simply under-regulate, their emotions. All of the things we discussed in the last chapter about these emotions being messengers and motivators are just as true here. However, approaching them can look a little different than the open space we talked about since we need to increase regulation rather than connection to our emotions. In this chapter, we'll discuss what can cause our emotions to feel so uncontained; we'll also touch on how to contain them in healthy, adaptive ways that still allow us to maximize their utility as messengers and motivators.

Root Causes of Emotional Dysregulation

When that tantrum starts—whether it's in us or someone else—it can feel like a mystery. It may feel out-of-the-blue and perhaps even out-of-control. We'll address exactly how to appropriately control these uncontained emotions in a minute. But first, what drives them? We'll hit on a few of the root causes of this emotional dysregulation here.

First, we sometimes take our emotions *too* seriously. That's right—it is possible to overly emphasize our emotions. As we discussed in the last chapter, emotions aren't facts. They also aren't permanent. Sometimes we forget these things, letting our emotions completely define us and our sense of reality. In these moments, we tend to let our thoughts run away too, telling us all kinds of stories about our emotions. We tend to feel, for example, as if we will be sad forever and come up with all kinds of reasons to explain our sadness (e.g., being "pushed around" or "overlooked" by others). All of a sudden, our emotions seem 10 or even 100 times bigger than when they started.

Dr. Puff: "I remember breaking up with my high school sweetheart in college. Like most people when they lose their first love, I felt very down and confused when we broke up. Although these are normal reactions, I can see in retrospect that I definitely let the feelings run away with me. I let them consume me, feeling as if my life was over without her. My thoughts followed right along, telling me stories about how we were *supposed* to be together and refusing to come up with a future that didn't include her. I thought about the break-up constantly. I was so unable to let the relationship go that I pursued a repeat relationship with my ex…twice! Now I can see that I just prolonged our pain (unnecessarily because we really weren't a good match anyway), but at the time my emotions were so unregulated that they really took both of us for a ride. I didn't find freedom until I was able to let go of all the stories I was telling myself about what the emotions meant, put the feelings in perspective as something very difficult *that would pass*, and move on with the present."

Dr. Puff's example illustrates how quickly our emotions can carry us away if we put too much emphasis on them, acting as if they are facts that define us and our lives. In fact, Dr. Puff's story is an example of a thinking error that many people get stuck in—it's called *catastophizing.* Yes, losing a love is difficult. For Dr. Puff, however, it felt like the end of the world, so he refused to accept it. Although understandable, this only made it harder and longer for him to grieve the relationship. Other thinking errors, like *personalizing* incidents (i.e., making everything in life, including perhaps our co-worker's sour expression, about us) and *black-and-white thinking* (i.e., feeling that things are either good or bad, right or wrong, all the time), can also heighten our emotions unnecessarily. Although it's outside the scope of this chapter to develop all of these patterns fully, suffice it to say that they often feed the negative stories we tell ourselves and foster our overly intense, unregulated, emotions reactions.

These unregulated, emotional reactions are often fed further by unspoken expectations. We all have hopes, desires, and even expectations about how life will go. Sometimes we determine these hopes and expectations, and sometimes society sets them for us. For example, we may *expect* to get married (and probably stay married), have kids, or get promoted one day. When life doesn't live up to these standards, our reactions may be extra intense because it feels as if life has wronged us or otherwise violated the rules somehow. These feeling are usually implicit and unspoken, making our reactions seem mysteriously intense.

Similarly, unresolved emotional wounds can also make our reactions seem mysteriously intense. We've all been hurt, let down, betrayed—you name it, we experience the gamut. A lot of people don't know how to deal with these emotions, so they simply try to stuff them. Unfortunately, stuffing doesn't work. Why? Because these "stuffed" emotions don't usually disappear or diminish with time. Instead, they stay stuffed and leak out in other situations. For example, perhaps our break-up is particularly difficult because of a previous break-up (or even other loss, like the death of a loved one) that we haven't fully processed. In this case, the unresolved emotions from our previous difficulties are likely to bubble up and come out when they are triggered by these current circumstances. It's true: Unresolved emotions don't go away; instead, they often come back in more intense reactions later.

Although we could continue, hopefully it is clear that there are a number of things that lead to mysteriously intense and even unregulated emotional reactions. These reactions are fed by past experiences, unspoken expectations about life, and even underlying patterns of responding to our emotions and circumstances. At their core, all of these difficulties have a common element of lacking skill in dealing with difficult emotions. Sadly, such skills do not come naturally at birth. Like any skill, from knitting to tennis to financial management, emotional management must be learned. In an ideal environment, it's picked up naturally through good modeling and parenting by our caretakers. In a lot of families, however, it's a lost art that we can easily leave home without. Hence, intense, emotional dysregulation is usually fostered by a lack of skill in dealing with emotions as much as by thinking errors, unmet expectations, or even past wounds.

5 Steps to Emotional Regulation

In the midst of the bleak landscape presented above, there is good news: It's never too late to learn the skills we need for emotional regulation. No matter where we start, these skills can help us to overcome thinking errors, unmet expectations, past wounds, or anything else causing our emotional reactions to seem out-of-control and overwhelming. Here are five basic steps to follow in developing the skill to regulate one's emotions:

1) Take it down a notch: When our emotions are unregulated and too intense, the first thing we need to do is calm down. It's physically impossible to think clearly when our hormones are raging or our bodies are otherwise reacting to a high level of emotionality. Hence, we need to physically take it down a notch by sitting down and taking some deep breaths. We want to turn our short, shallow breaths into deep, long ones. To lengthen them, it can be helpful to count slowly while breathing and try to make each breath a little longer. To deepen them, it's often useful to place one's hand on the stomach (rather than the chest) to make sure it's rising and falling with each breath. These tools can help us to physiologically calm down enough to begin thinking clearly again.

2) Create some distance: As our deep breathing takes effect, our brains may clear enough to allow us to move in another direction. And, yes, this is sometimes exactly what we need—a break from the intense situation and emotions. There are a number of things we can do to distract ourselves enough to take this break. Physical activity, such as running or yoga, is often helpful. Social activity, such as calling a friend or even walking around the mall, can also be effective. Even things that distract our minds, like movies or books, can be useful. It's important to try different activities, as what works for one person may not work for another. Once we know what activities work for us, it can be helpful to write them down on some sort of resource card that can be pulled out in the intense situations when one's brain is no longer thinking clearly. Engaging in these activities then helps one cope with and distract from the intense, overwhelming feelings.

3) Soothe with the mind and body: Although the distraction will usually help us calm down, sometimes we need a little more. Intense emotions can simply leave us feeling incredibly riled up and even off-kilter or otherwise not quite ourselves. At such times, there are a number of intentional practices that can help soothe and re-ground us. Mental practices, such as meditation, may create appropriate calmness and distance from the intense emotions. Positive self-talk—i.e., reassuring statements, such as "it will be okay" or "this situation is only temporary"—can also be soothing. In addition to these cognitive practices, engaging the body can be very grounding. The best way to approach this is to creatively engage the five senses. For example, squeeze a stress ball, stare at a lit candle, or slowly rub some good smelling lotion onto one's arms. Really focusing on these activities (whether they are done one at a time or all together) can help soothe and re-ground us physiologically and emotionally. In this way, both the body and the mind can provide further soothing for our intense emotions.

4) Return when ready: Once we are sufficiently soothed and grounded, it's important to eventually return and reflect on the situation that got us so riled up in the first place. The goal, after all, is not to get rid of our feelings, but to calm down enough that we can use them effectively as the messengers and motivators they are meant to be. Hence, after being sufficiently distracted and soothed—whether this takes 20 minutes or 2 days, it's important to plan a time to sit quietly and reflect upon what happened. What triggered the intense emotional reaction? What stories or thinking errors did it generate? What were the real messages behind the emotions, and how can they be most appropriately acted upon? This sort of self check-in should probably be time-limited (e.g., one, targeted hour rather than consuming our thoughts all day). Short, focused time will make it possible for us to gain the available benefits from our emotions rather than be carried away by them.

5) Repeat...and get help as needed! The reality is that we can sometimes get riled up all over again—either because we are reflecting on the situation or because something new happens. At these times, it's important to return to steps one through three, taking deep breaths and doing things to intentionally distract and soothe. Many people may find that they need help with this process too. That's okay. These skills were meant to be learned in relationship and are sometimes most easily engaged with others. When one is getting stuck again and again on any of these steps, it's probably time to turn to an emotionally intelligent friend or an actual professional (e.g., therapists) for help. Others can sometimes help us gain new perspective and traction that we simply lack alone. The point is that there is no shame in getting stuck or reaching out; the important thing is to build the skills, regardless of how one gets there.

Managing the Big Three

Before we move on to actually practicing emotional regulation, we'd like to take special note of what we call "the big three." These are the three most difficult emotions for most people to manage. We are pretty good at dealing with things like happiness, but we have more trouble when it comes to sadness, anger, and fear. Like all of our emotions, these three are messengers and motivators that are meant to help us. Unlike the others, however, they can feel particularly intimidating and out-of-control. Hence, we'd like to touch briefly on each of these emotions to remove some of the mystery and intimidation.

First, *sadness* is an indicator that we feel some type of pain or loss. It may be accompanied by things like physical tiredness, changes in appetite, crying, lack of motivation, and difficulty concentrating. Sadness is meant to move us toward grieving and comfort. It can be helpful to approach sadness in a way that allows us to grieve, such as journaling or talking to (and, yes, perhaps even crying with) a friend. Although painful and tiring, this experience should feel relieving and even healing over time. If it doesn't, we probably have something else going on here. Perhaps we haven't really been able to connect with the source of our sadness. Alternatively, maybe our mind is simply running away with inaccurate stories that have nothing to do with actual loss. These stuck moments are definitely a time to follow steps one through five above, including possibly getting help from a professional. Overall, the important point is that sadness is meant to be healing, enabling us to grieve our losses and move toward comfort and restoration.

Dr. White: "Sadness is an emotion I've had to learn to deal with in my adulthood. As a child, I just tried to stuff it…and ended up depressed. As an adult, I had to learn that it was meant to be *good* and *helpful.* Although I didn't like it at first (and I'd still prefer joy!), I've learned to embrace and lean into my sadness. Recently, for example, I had a significant loss in my life. I felt sad pretty continuously for a week or two after, and I continue to notice pockets of sadness popping up at occasional, often unexpected times. When this happens, I try to take some time to journal or even sit and cry with someone I trust. I allow myself to feel the sadness of the loss. I'm usually tired when I'm done, but I also oddly feel some relief. Plus, I notice that the sadness has gotten much smaller as I've leaned into the feeling over time. This is different, however, than just coming home from a long day and feeling tired and overwhelmed. At those times, I've learned that if I lean too deeply into my feelings, my mind just runs away with all kinds of stories. What I need at those moments is simply a little distraction and a soothing, good nights rest. Hence, it's been huge for me to learn to discern when my sadness reflects legitimate loss (versus plain dysregulation) and lean in accordingly."

The second difficult emotion is *anger.* Anger is an indicator that we perceive some sort of attack or injustice. It may be accompanied by things like a racing heart, tense muscles, changes in body temperature, and shallow breathing; some people also feel like punching something, while others may be more inclined to cry. Anger is meant to help us assert and protect both ourselves and those we love. It is critical to process anger in contained ways that do not hurt people or property. Hence, good options are often physical activities, like running or martial arts, which release some of the pent up energy. Sitting in a private place and yelling out the frustrations, writing an angry letter (which will usually NOT be sent), or tearing up some paper can also be helpful. As with sadness, these activities should be relieving and healing. If they're not, we probably have something else going on—perhaps some more crazy stories or maybe even some deeper emotions (e.g., sadness, fear) that are actually driving our anger. If this is the case, yelling or tearing paper may make our anger feel more intense; then we definitely need to return to steps one through five above, again likely culminating in getting help. Like sadness, anger should also feel healing and protective if regulated and processed appropriately.[5]

The last of the big three is *fear*. We could probably also add *anxiety* here. Fear and anxiety are indicators that we perceive some sort of danger. They are often accompanied by feelings similar to those described above with anger—a racing heart, tense muscles, and shallow breathing. Fear is meant to help us react to danger by fighting, fleeing, or freezing. If one is actually in danger, it's definitely best to lean into these responses. Most of the time, however, fear and anxiety arise with perceived dangers that are not real. Our minds are constantly looking for threats and often perceive things (often future things) that are not really a current reality or threat. When that's the case, it's important to follow steps one through five above, calming ourselves so that we can think clearly and then identify what is really scaring us. Once we've clearly identified our fear, we can sometimes easily see that it's irrational and effectively soothe ourselves with reassuring phrases. Sometimes, especially with more chronic fears, we also need to work toward reducing the

---

[5] For more help on discerning and processing anger appropriately, see Dr. Puff's book "Anger Work: How to Express Your Anger and Still Be Kind" under "Publications" on his website (www.doctorpuff.com).

fear by facing it head on, which is a great place to again get help. Hence, although it sometimes carries us away, fear is actually meant to protect us from danger.

The bottom line is that all of "the big three"—sadness, anger, and fear—are meant to be helpful. Sadness can heal loss, while anger and fear can protect us and our loved ones from harm. Sometimes these emotions do run away with us, creating all kinds of dysregulation. At those moments, it's important to use our breathing, distracting, and soothing to calm ourselves (i.e., steps 1-3 above). Only then can we lean into the feelings and process them appropriately (i.e., step 4 above). Overall, now that we've described the purpose of "the big three" as well as the initial path for dealing with them, we hope they can be more easily processed without so much mystery or intimidation.

Putting It into Practice

In fact, we hope this entire chapter has taken some of the mystery and intimidation out of intense, seemingly out-of-control emotions. We've talked about how these emotions can arise from a number of places, including habitual patterns of overemphasizing our feelings, thinking errors that engage crazy stories about our feelings, unspoken expectations, and unresolved wounds. All of these experiences are normal, yet none of them need to control us.

It is possible to develop the skills to regulate and utilize our emotions in helpful ways. Specifically, we need to learn to calm, distract, soothe, reflect, and get help as needed. These steps can even help with regulating and processing "the big three"—sadness, anger, and fear. As we learn to use these skills with our intense emotions, we will be increasingly able to contain the out-of-control, tantruming child within.

Today, we'd like to invite you to start this process by choosing one emotion that is particularly challenging for you. Take a moment to think through "the big three." Which one tends to carry you away into uncontained, dysregulated emotions the most? When you've chosen the emotion, get a 3x5 index card and write "When I'm feeling ____ (your chosen emotion)" at the top of it. We will make this a resource card to help you contain your intense, chosen emotion.

Like the sample on the next page, your job is create a plan for what you will do when you feel that emotion. You can copy the sample word for word, filling in the underlined portions with your own plan. When you get to the sections for distracting and soothing (#2 & 3), go back and read the portion above that talks about the kind of activities and statements that can be distracting and soothing. Then think back to times when you have felt the emotion before: What helped you to calm down? As long as these were safe and healthy activities (e.g., walking, not drinking), list them on your card. You may also need to try out new activities at times when you're feeling the emotion to see what is actually helpful for you. If you get stumped, ask other people what they do when they feel that emotion and try out the ideas that are safe and healthy. Take your time in listing things that you know actually work for you. Make sure you have a number of them and that they are things you can do in the moment (e.g., not skiing unless you live next to a slope and it's winter!).

Once you've completed your list of distracting and soothing activities, list people under step five that you know could help you if you got stuck. These should be people who are emotionally intelligent, caring, and (at least sometimes) available. They should not be a critical family member or emotionally avoidant friend. If you can't think of anyone, it may be time to make new friends or even enlist the help of a professional. Once you have completed your card, keep it in your purse or wallet. Next time you are feeling your emotion, pull out your card and use it. Then return and answer the questions for reflection below.

Sample Resource Card

When I'm feeling sad…

1) Take long, deep breaths!

2) Distract by reading a book, going for a walk, napping, or calling a friend.

3) Soothe by taking a bath, lighting a candle, or looking at and describing artwork. Also, remind myself, "This sadness is only temporary" and "I'm going to be okay."

4) Return to my feeling when I'm ready and ask what triggered it, what the message is, and how I can respond appropriately.

5) Get help as needed from Sally, John, or a therapist.

Questions for Reflection

1) What was easiest and most difficult about *completing* my resource card?

2) What was easiest and most difficult about *using* my resource card?

3) What do my answers above tell me about myself (e.g., I'm good at distracting, but not asking for help)?

4) Was I able to successfully complete the five steps for my chosen emotion? If not, what obstacles did I encounter?

5) What are my next steps in building skills that can help me overcome these obstacles (e.g., practice, contacting a therapist)?

Tip #12: Remember Your Higher Power

Although they are not religious groups, Alcoholics Anonymous and other 12-step groups begin with the idea that we are powerless to solve our own problems and must turn to a Higher Power for help. Every newcomer who joins the groups must begin by owning these truths. Why? Because spirituality is a critical, yet easily overlooked, piece of our health and well-being.

It's true—in the midst of our fast-paced, fit-in-all-in world, it is very easy to lose track of our spirituality. When it comes to stocking our empty pantries or spending time in prayer, the practical tasks and errands often win out. Our spiritual beliefs and practices end up taking a back seat to all of our other priorities and tasks, becoming something that does not fit in our schedule…or something that we are too tired to engage in when we finally "find" the time. After awhile, our spirituality can seem so distant that it may even begin to feel irrelevant to our lives. Our lives are so full and busy that some people give up their spiritual practices, while others give up their spiritual beliefs all together.

Although understandable, we let go of our spirituality at our own risk and detriment. Remembering our Higher Power is critical because it provides a sense of meaning, connection, peace, purpose, and perspective that is vital to our health. We may all have different beliefs about the name and characteristics of our Higher Power, but it's important for our emotional well-being that we keep our Higher Power in mind regardless. The point of this chapter is not to espouse any one religious belief, but to instead remind us all why our spirituality matters and to help us make space for it in our lives.

Establishing Meaning & Connection

The biggest and most foundational benefit of spirituality is that it provides a sense of meaning. We all have so many big questions: Why are we here? What is the purpose of life? Why do "bad" things happen to "good" people? What happens after we die? These are core questions for us as human beings—whether or not we actually allocate time to think about them in our daily lives. The first benefit of remembering our spirituality is that we find answers to these questions.

Finding answers to these questions is not only helpful in itself—it also provides us an important sense of connection. First and foremost, we are connected to our Higher Power. For some, this is a deeply intimate relationship, while, for others, it is a more intellectual presence. Either way, it is vastly comforting to know we are not alone, and we have a connection to something greater than ourselves. For those who ascribe to some sort of popular or organized spirituality, we also gain a sense of connection to a spiritual community. We find like-minded people with similar beliefs and values with whom we can journey through life. Hence, as we answer the questions of life, we find connection to both our Higher Power and others who have found similar answers.

Before we move on, let's take a second with one important question: Who cares? Why does it matter if we answer the big questions of life or connect to something bigger than ourselves? Indeed, these things can feel superfluous at times when everything in our lives is on-track and moving along well. But what happens when we have a child who is born with a birth defect or struggling with a mental illness? What do we do when we are diagnosed with a chronic or fatal illness? How do we cope when a loved one is robbed or murdered? When life gets difficult, it is critical that we have a sense of meaning and connection to fall back on. The meaning and connection we gain from our spirituality fight the alienation and meaningless of life—in both good times and bad—thus increasing our resiliency and overall well-being.

Engaging the 3 P's: Perspective, Purpose, & Peace

In addition to giving us a sense of meaning and connection, our spirituality also provides three important "P's": Perspective, purpose, and peace. The first "P," *perspective*, refers to the idea that our spirituality gives us a new way to look at ourselves and our lives. It allows us a new lens through which we can view our circumstances, or at least a bigger picture that extends beyond ourselves.

An old Chinese proverb illustrates the idea of perspective well. The story goes that a farmer and his son lose their one horse one day. Neighbors come and offer sympathy at the family's bad luck, but the farmer seems unperturbed and simply states, "We'll see." Sure enough, the son goes out looking for the horse later than week…and finds four more wild horses to add to their stock! Now the neighbors come by, offering their congratulations at the family's great luck. Again, the farmer seems unshaken, stating again, "We'll see." The next day, his son breaks his leg while training the new, wild horses. Seeing that the son is unable to help around the farm, the neighbors again offer their sympathy. The farmer again replies, "We'll see." Then, the following week, the emperor comes with a document conscripting every able-bodied young man into immediate military service. The son is exempt because of his broken leg! Again, the farmer's only response is "We'll see." This farmer's outlook is different from his neighbors because he looks at life through a broader and longer-term perspective that takes into account the impermanence of daily circumstances. Although our beliefs may or may not align with this farmer, our spirituality can help us to gain our own varied and broader perspectives from which to view life.

Just as these new lenses may provide a renewed or varied sense of perspective, they also impact our ideas about *purpose*. We all want a sense of meaning—not only in life as a whole, but in who we are and what we do. We want to answer the questions, "Who am I?" and "Why am I here?" We hope to be remembered when we are gone and leave a positive legacy behind for those who will follow us. Our spirituality often helps us to answer these questions and gain direction in our legacy.

> *Dr. Puff:* "I began my spiritual quest in my young adolescence. At first, this quest literally took me across the USA in search of answers. Later, my quest led me to explore spiritual gurus and giants. Through it all, a nagging sense of needing to answer life's questions, particularly the question of 'Who, or what, am I?' kept pushing me forward. When I went to graduate school, psychology helped to lessen the struggle that haunted me with these questions, but it did not extinguish it. I ultimately had to find these answers through my spirituality. Eventually, I had a real spiritual awakening that opened my eyes to the non-duality of life. From then on, I felt a sense of lightness and peace instead of struggle and even lingering depression. This shift came from finally answering the questions, 'What is life all about?' and 'Who am I in the midst of it?' It also gave me a new sense of purpose in helping others to find these answers and experience the same sense of being free and home that I've found."[6]

As Dr. Puff's story demonstrates, our spirituality can provide us a sense of perspective, purpose, and even *peace*. That's right—as we answer the big questions and gain a new perspective on our circumstances and ourselves, we also gain a deepened sense of peace. Suddenly, the big questions no longer haunt us. We have

---

[6] For those interested in learning more about Dr. Puff's spiritual awakening, check out his Enlightenment podcasts and/or his book "Spiritual Enlightenment: Awakening to the Supreme Reality"—both found on his website at www.doctorpuff.com.

a sense of assurance regarding our place in the world. What's more, we know that life is not all about us, so we don't have to control everything so tightly. Instead, we can say, "Thy will be done," and simply let go, enjoying what is. No, these are not always immediate or easy shifts. Nonetheless, the perspective, purpose, and peace that our spirituality can provide has immense benefits for our overall health and well-being.

Leaning In

So how do we tap into all of these immense benefits of spirituality? Simple: We lean in. First, we lean in figure out what we really believe. Some of us avoid this search, simply swallowing our spirituality wholeheartedly from our parents…or rejecting it out of turn and ignoring spirituality altogether. Sometimes we claim that we're just too busy and, "We'll get to it later." Our advice is: Don't wait! Figuring out your spirituality will lead to greater health now and less regrets later. Hence, ask your questions and seek for answers—it's worth it now and in the end.

> *Dr. White:* "I did not grow up in any particular religious tradition. In high school, however, I had some friends who took me to church…and I pretty much swallowed their faith whole. The newness and excitement of the shift was initially very satisfying. By college, however, I began to have some spiritually 'dry' seasons for a couple of years that caused me to question my faith and journey. I tried to avoid these

questions and push harder into my spirituality—only to end up feeling more 'dry' and even depressed. Finally, my senior year, I took the time to lean in. I read tons of books and talked to lots of people, trying to understand various perspectives—including both those I shared and those that were drastically different. I even wrote a 110-page paper sorting out all my thoughts and ideas. Eventually, I came back around to my original faith; however, this time I had an unbelievably new assurance and peace that came with really asking and deeply answering the questions for myself. Since then, those answers have sustained me, providing perspective, peace, purpose, and more—regardless of how my spirituality makes me feel on any given day or season."

As Dr. White's story illustrates, leaning into our spirituality can help us to glean the benefits spirituality has to offer. For some, like Dr. White, this may mean leaning into questions and seeking answers. For others whose answers feel more solidified, leaning in may involve actually being involved in one's faith. It may be making time for spiritual activities, like prayer or service. It may also involve connecting to others who share similar beliefs to gain a sense of community. A healthy spirituality should improve both our life and the lives of those around us as we engage with it. Sometimes we have to get creative in how this works for us—in our individual stages of life and with our particular personalities. Nonetheless, leaning in to both find answers and engage with our spirituality will allow us to reap all of the rich benefits it can provide.

Putting It into Practice

Bottomline? Our spirituality matters. Having a healthy heart and an overall, holistic well-being involves maximizing the spiritual aspect of ourselves as well as the emotional, physical, etc. Why? Because our spirituality provides a sense of meaning, connection, perspective, purpose, and peace that transcends us and the other areas of our being. No deep connection to our bodies or others can substitute for the immense benefits we gain here. Hence, it's time to lean in—seeking answers to our questions, engaging with our beliefs/communities, and otherwise remembering our Higher Power.

To begin, we challenge you to complete the chart on the next page. Starting with the first box, rate yourself on a scale of 0-10 (0 being "not at all" and 10 being "completely and perfectly"). Remember, no one will see these answers except you, so it's okay to take your time and be honest. Then take the action suggested based on your scores. As always, return to answer the questions for reflection when you're done.

How thoroughly have I answered the big questions of life (e.g., "Who am I?" "What happens after I die?")?
Rating (0-10): ______

Score of 6 or below

Stop! It's time to take a spiritual quest of your own! Get out a journal and write down your questions about life, purpose, etc. Then figure out one step you will take (e.g., reading a book, talking to someone) to begin engaging with these questions.

Score of 7+

How confident am I about my answers?
Rating (0-10): ______

Score of 6 or below

Stop! It's time to address the insecurity in your spiritual journey. Begin by getting out a journal and honestly writing down any and all doubts, concerns, or issues that come up about your spirituality. Then plan a time to meet with a spiritual leader and discuss these thoughts.

Score of 7+

How engaged am I with my spirituality, gaining meaning, connection, perspective, etc.?
Rating (0-10): __

Score of 6 or below

Stop! It's time to re-engage with your spirituality. Take a minute and think about what's missing—connection to a spiritual community? Spiritual practices? Plan one step you will take in the next week to move you closer to these missing aspects.

Note: Scores of 7 or above on the third scale are a sign of a strong spirituality. If this is you, go out and enjoy, celebrating what you have in this area of your life!

Questions for Reflection

1) Did any of my answers above surprise me? Why or why not?

2) If I scored a 6 or below on any of the three rating scales, is there something that happened to derail me in my spiritual journey?

3) What obstacles or challenges may I face in renewing my spiritual journey? How can I overcome them?

4) If I scored a 7 or above on all three questions, what led me to have such a rich and satisfying spiritual life? Are there any ways others can benefit from my experience?

5) Overall, what do I hope to gain from my spirituality? Also, how close am I to this goal, and what steps can I take to get closer?

Tying It All Together

In this section, we've tried to paint a balanced picture of the heart. The picture starts with recognizing that the heart matters. Our emotions are actually meant to be good and helpful, while ignoring them often leads to a myriad of problems over time. Hence, it behooves us to learn to listen to our emotional cues, using them as messages about what's happening both inside and outside of us. The messages aren't always fun and sometimes they can be a bit confusing to sort through, but they really are meant to be helpful to us as both messengers and motivators. We can begin to tap into this resource by creating some space, intentionally connecting to our emotions, and sorting through their message; this, in fact, is what it means to *mind the messenger.*

Of course, we don't want to be overrun by this messenger. And, yes, sometimes we do have some pretty intense emotions that might feel overwhelming. There are a number of places from which these intense emotions can arise, such as thinking errors, unspoken expectations, and unresolved wounds. In spite of these patterns and others, however, we can learn to regulate our emotions such that their messages remain helpful to us rather than overwhelming. We achieve this regulation by engaging in specific activities to calm, distract, soothe, reflect, and seek help. Over time, these steps allow us to appropriately *contain the child* within.

Once we are able to both contain and mind our emotions, we are able to tap into the richness and helpfulness they provide in life. In reality, though, this picture it still incomplete without our spirituality. Whatever we specifically believe, our spirituality has the power to transcend us, connecting us to things that are bigger than ourselves. Overall, our spirituality adds to our emotional well-being in creating a sense of meaning, connection, perspective, purpose, and peace. That's why it's critical to *remember our Higher Power.*

Although the heart can feel pretty confusing to a lot of people, these three pieces really can provide us access to the richness that the heart provides. Each piece may sound simple, yet it can definitely take some serious practice to develop these skills in life. Nonetheless, they are worth it, for they allow us to fully utilize our hearts without being overrun by them. In other words, we can tap into the abandon and passion of that carefree, dancing child without losing the controlled skill of the master.

Part V: Relationships

In addition to feeling passion, having focus, and being in good shape, a dancer must also be aware of and considering his partner(s). Just like with heart, a dancer may display an immense amount of skill, yet the dance will still look off and perhaps fall flat if he can't connect with others who are dancing alongside him. Simply imagine a man who is a fantastic dancer…yet cannot effectively lead a partner. No matter how many moves he has mastered, he will still find the actual dance extremely difficult. The same would be true of a female dancer who knew tons of moves but couldn't follow her partner. It turns out that how dancers move with others can be as critical as how they move overall.

In this area, the skill of the master probably trumps the spontaneity of the child. After all, the child can get away with completely ignoring those around her, and maybe even stepping on a few toes, without it immediately ruining the beauty of the dance. The same is not necessarily true of the master. We expect masters to be perfectly coordinated and graceful—individually and with others. And, yes, this is true whether a dancer is performing a tango, a group ballet, or almost any other kind of dance. The master must be able to coordinate and pair well with others in order to really succeed in the dance.

Clearly, the same is true of life. We can be fantastic at staying in shape, great at succeeding in our career, excellent at living with focus…and yet still struggle immensely if we cannot coordinate our movements with others. And, unlike the carefree child, life doesn't have as much grace with adults who ignore others or frequently step on their toes. Whether we are talking about partners, friends, family, children, co-workers, or others, this is a relational world. In order to do well in it, we must know how to move well with others.

The exciting part of this is that relationships can be a great source of meaning, satisfaction, and more when they are functioning well. For those who frequently struggle in relationships, this may sound kind of strange. Perhaps relationships in general—or specific ones, like the romantic kind—have been more of a source of pain and heartache. It may sound bizarre, then, to emphasize how much relationships can be a source of intimacy and beauty. Nonetheless, this is exactly what we contend. This section will begin to birth or increase such intimacy and beauty by discussing how to form, maintain, and protect good relationships. As we master these three keys, we can soon be moving in sync with our partners, just like the most skilled dancers out there.

Tip #13: Form a Good Team

Athletes know something that the rest of us sometimes miss: To win, we need a good team. It's not enough to be a stellar figure skater if our partner is going to fall on his butt as soon as he gets on the ice. It will only take us so far to be the best soccer goalie in the world if our team can't score at the other end of the field. Even being the best gymnast may win us some medals, but our team will still lose if the other gymnasts can't pull their weight. Truly, sports emphasize the importance of teamwork.

Whether we like it or not, life also tends to emphasize the importance of teamwork. Even when we think life is about what we can accomplish on our own, our team matters in the end. How our co-workers do their job influences the success of our projects and company, thus creating security and success for our job. How our partners treat us and aid in the care of our homes and children impacts our attitudes and time. Even how our friends and family live influences what we do in our free time. Although we may or may not be quite as comfortable with it, life is characterized by teamwork just like sports.

It's critical that we recognize the importance of teamwork and use it to influence our lives positively. Just as there are lots of drills we can run to improve the skills of our athletic teams, there are lots of things we can do to invest in our relationships and make them better; we'll discuss some of these in upcoming chapters. For now, we'll focus on the reality that, just like with sports, one of the most important ingredients for winning teams is connecting with other dedicated, talented people from the start. If we try to form a soccer team with a bunch of novices or couch potatoes, we may improve over time but we're not likely to be competing for the Olympics anytime soon! Consequently, we'll begin with how we can form a good, solid team from the start by both being and finding good teammates.

Step 1: Be a Good Teammate

The first step in creating healthy teams is *being* a good teammate. We don't often like to start here, particularly when it comes to romantic relationships. It's simply easier to point the finger elsewhere. For example, we are single because "there are no good men out there." Or, we're in an unhappy marriage because "our partner ____________ *(fill in the blank: doesn't communicate, spends too much time away from home, etc.)*." There is often some validity to these claims. At the same time, however, pointing the finger outside of ourselves usually doesn't represent the whole story.

Representing the whole relational story must include every person in the relationship. Seem obvious? Of course! Yet it is often difficult to notice our contribution to our singleness, unhappy marriage, difficult friendships, etc. Noticing our contribution may mean owning that we aren't actively looking for a partner, or perhaps we have some unresolved issues that cause us to shy away from relationships when they get too vulnerable. Alternatively, maybe our partner doesn't communicate with us (at least in part) because we yell or withdraw every time he/she tries. Relationships are never one-sided. Understanding them fully must involve seeing and owning our part as well as the other person's.

> *Dr. White:* "I was single throughout high school and college. At the time, I would have volunteered quickly that I wanted to be in a relationship and simply wasn't finding any good, quality guys who were interested. There was definitely truth in that statement. However, I went through a long process of soul-searching after college which caused me to realize that on some level I really didn't want to be in a relationship. I was too scared—scared to be vulnerable, scared to be hurt, scared of all the unknowns. I had to work through these fears—and even the reasons behind them, like my parents' divorce—before I was really ready to date. This was a long process, and yet, lo and behold, my husband was easy to find as soon as I made it through the other side. There probably are girls out there who really are single because they aren't finding quality guys; however, for me and many others, there are things we were/are contributing to missing these guys and the relationships they have to offer too."

As Dr. White's story illustrates, there are two sides to every story, particularly those about relationships. Hence, it's as critical to *be* a good teammate as it is to find good teammates. So how do we become a good teammate? Try the following:

~*Be the partner you want:* The most important step toward being a good teammate is acting like the partner, friend, etc. we want to have. Want someone who communicates? Start communicating. Hope to have relationships with others who are physically fit or healthy? Go work out or learn how to cook healthy. Sometimes these steps involve learning new skills (like communication), while other times they just involve forming new habits (like eating healthier). Either way, the idea here is to act like the partner, friend, etc. we would like to have. This will do two things: 1) It will attract more people who practice the same positive, healthy things in their lives; 2) It will elicit new, more positive reactions from those with whom we already have relationships. Truly, being the partner or friend we hope for is the most important step to finding the "right" person; this step also helps us to create the healthy relationships we desire with those who are already in our lives.

~*Work through unresolved issues:* As we attempt to be the partner or friend we want, we may notice places we fail. Perhaps we want a good communicator, so we try to communicate better ourselves…only to find ourselves withdrawing or flying into a rage. When we find ourselves unable to act like the partner or friend we want, we need to figure out what skill deficits or unresolved wounds are creating these difficulties and deal with them. This step often takes help from others—friends, therapists, etc. That's okay. We're trying to be good relational partners, and the easiest place to learn that is through relationships. Whether we do it alone or with others, working through unresolved issues is often difficult, yet it's a critical step to becoming a good teammate.

~Ask friends and family: Another great way to be a good teammate is to ask friends or family how we can be a better friend, spouse, etc. What can we work on or do for them that would make them more satisfied in the relationship? Unless one is in an abusive relationship, this question can help us to get on the right track in becoming a better teammate. It is also particularly useful when we get stumped. Perhaps we can't think of issues we need to work on or things we need to change. In that case, our friends and family may be able to give us feedback about where (if any place) we're going wrong and getting stuck.[7] It may be difficult to ask, and we certainly need to be wise about whom and when we ask, but our friends and family can often give us useful feedback about being a better teammate.

---

[7] Two important caveats are needed here: (1) Never ask cruel or abusive friends or family what else you can do to be a better friend, partner, etc.—they'll only respond with more cruelty and abuse! In this case, what's needed is actually more boundaries and new teammates. (2) There are certainly some instances in which we really have done all we can to be a good teammate and we simply can't find a partner, or the one we have is refusing to meet us half way; we don't rule this possibility out, but merely say it is the exception. If all of one's friends, family, and particularly an objective third-party (e.g., a therapist or spiritual leader) agree we have done all we can, then that may very well be true.

Step 2: Find Good Teammates

Once we are really on the path to being a better teammate, we need to make sure we find good teammates too. Of course, there may already be people in our lives, like family our spouses, that we either never picked or chose long ago. Simply being a good teammate will elicit the best in them as well. For those of us still looking for new friends or partners, however, we need to be intentional to find good teammates. As we noted above, this is likely to be easier and more natural when we are being a good teammate. But what else can we do to ensure we find the relationships we're looking for? Consider the following:

~Look for like-minded people: Ideally, we want to find people with similar values, interests, beliefs, etc. Whether we are talking about spirituality or physical fitness, people who are like-minded will support and lead us closer to our goals, while people with very contrasting beliefs and values may move us away from them. Hence, as we're forming new relationships, it's critical to ask what really matters to each one of us. Once we figure out what's most important, this can help us figure out where to search for like-minded people. For example, if what's most important to us is spirituality, church would be a great place to start looking. If, in contrast, what's most important is being a mom, perhaps some sort of mother's group would be a great place to begin. There are no right answers to what's important to each one of us; the critical thing is to simply be discerning about finding people who

will help us to become more of who we want to be rather than taking us away from our goals and values.

Dr. Puff: "I resonate with the importance and power of finding positive, like-minded people. I began making significant changes to my lifestyle as I was finishing Princeton and starting a new graduate program. Initially, I was able to enjoy these changes with my classmates in my graduate program. For example, as I wanted to be more active and outdoors, I found that they would go hiking with me. As we got busier with our program, however, they stopped making time for this pursuit. Eventually, I had to join a hiking club to find other people who were like-minded in wanting to prioritize being active and outdoors. The people I met in this club actually helped me to maintain my new, healthy habits and even encouraged me to eat healthier too. Overall, I was struck by the power of having like-minded people around: They can help us stick to what's important to us; make it more enjoyable along the way; and sometimes even move us toward new, positive changes as well."

~Notice the impact of the relationship: As Dr. Puff's story illustrates, it's important that we are discerning about the impact of the relationships around us. When we are hanging out with that other person, do we feel inspired or exhausted? After we leave, do we feel encouraged or disheartened? The people we spend time

with have an enormous impact on us—whether or not we are aware of it. As a side note here, being attentive to the impact people have on us may cause us to realize particular family members or friends have an extremely negative impact. When that's the case, it may be time to set some boundaries or spend less time with that person in order to limit the negative impact. In other words, we can both notice and *act upon* the impact of the relationship—moving toward those who encourage us and away from those who bring us down.

~Trust community: Still not sure? Sometimes, particularly with dating, it can be tricky to discern exactly whether the person is a good or bad influence. Often the impact is complex or subtle, and it's hard to sort out. In that case, it can be helpful to turn to those around us—trusted friends or family, therapists, or spiritual leaders—to get their input into the quality of the relationship. When everyone around us is providing the same message about the impact and quality of the relationship, we can probably trust them to help guide us.

As we institute these steps to finding good teammates, we'll experience the immense benefits that come with them. We'll find people who uplift us and move us toward common goals and values rather than take us away from who and what we want to be. We may also find it's easier to get along with those around us because we share what we find really important. In other words, we'll find that it's easier to live healthy, positive lives. Finding like-minded people who influence us in positive directions is truly a great step toward forming a winning team.

Remember, It's Never Black-and White!

As we talk about forming a winning team, it's important to remember that most people and relationships are not black-and-white. At our best, we are simply moving toward becoming better, healthier versions of ourselves. The same is true of our relationships; at their best, they are continuing to evolve into something new and growth-producing. The point? We probably won't ever "arrive" as the perfect teammate—nor will our spouses, friends, or others.

This caveat is important to keep in mind in order to avoid a number of common errors in trying to form good teams, such as:

~Error #1 – Increasing Self-Criticism: It would be possible to take the information discussed above and use it to beat one's self up for not being a perfect teammate. We may begin to see all of our flaws and feel like a horrible person. This is NOT the point! The point is to be growing and moving forward, celebrating our strengths *and* our ability to work on our weaknesses.

~Error #2 – Judging Others: In a similar vein, it would be possible to take the information above and use it to increase our judgment of others. We might decide that because they don't share our same values, other people are both poor choices for us in intimate relationships *and* poor choices period. In reality, however, these are really not the same thing. It is very possible to decide that

someone isn't quite right for us without making them out to be bad.

~Error #3 – Categorizing Our Relationships as "Good" or "Bad": In addition to judging others, it may be tempting to use the information above to judge our relationships. We may try to categorize each one into "good" and "bad." Indeed, it is important to be discerning about the impact a relationship has on us. At the same time, though, most relationships are more complex than simply "good" or "bad." Most relationships are also in progress too, and can often be made better through our own efforts as well as the efforts of the other person.

These errors all have something important in common: They are a matter of perspective. Each error goes to the extreme, deciding that because we can see weaknesses, that person or relationship must be bad. It's critical, however, that we keep a balanced perspective as we work on our teams. Each one of us, as well as our friends, family, and relationships, probably has strengths and weaknesses. Like it or not, forming winning teams will involve holding this ambiguity as we move toward improving ourselves and our relationships.

Putting It into Practice

The bottom line is that this is a relational world in which we need good teams. The first step in forming good teams is being the best teammate possible. Even if we find the greatest people in the world, our relationships with them will still stink if we aren't good partners or friends. As a result, it's critical to deal with any unresolved issues and build up our own skills in order to be the friends, partners, etc. we'd like to have. As we discussed, friends and family can usually help direct us if we aren't sure where to start. Truly, being a good teammate is the best place to start in forming healthy relationships.

The second step in forming healthy relationships is finding like-minded people. The people around us tend to have an immense impact upon us. As a result, it's critical for us to be mindful and discerning regarding their influence, moving toward people who share our values and help us become more of who we want to be...and away from those who discourage us or take us in directions we don't want to go. This doesn't mean we need to categorize ourselves or others as "good" or "bad"; it simply means that we focus on building relationships with people who are the best fit for us. In this way, we can follow the smartest athletes in the world in being intentional about forming good teams from the start.

As we reflect on forming good teams with like-minded people, it's important to begin sorting through what we value most in the big areas of our lives. In other words, what do we value most in the cognitive, physical, emotional, relational, and professional realms? Take a few minutes and thoughtfully make a list of your top values here. Remember to consider each area of life; in this vein, your list might include anything from positive thinking to healthy eating or spending within your means. After you've made your list, take some time to answer the questions for reflection.

My top values:

1. ______________________________
2. ______________________________
3. ______________________________
4. ______________________________
5. ______________________________
6. ______________________________
7. ______________________________
8. ______________________________
9. ______________________________
10. ______________________________

Questions for Reflection

1) How easy or difficult was for me to identify my own values?

2) How do I live out these values in my own life?

3) Are there steps I need to take, such as building new skills or resolving old issues, to more effectively live out these values and thus be a good teammate?

4) Which of these values do the most significant people in my life share? Which ones do they not share?

5) Where can I find like-minded people who might share these missing values?

Tip #14: Keep Those Diamonds Shiny

Any woman who's ever been newly engaged, or anyone who's been around these new brides-to-be, knows how concerned the brides-to-be are with their hands. If ever there was a time for manicured nails, this is it! Why? Because both the bride and all of her loved ones will frequently be admiring the beautiful, new diamond engagement ring she wears. Not surprisingly, the ring is kept shiny at all costs, whether this means cleaning it twice a day or avoiding lotions and other substances that may diminish the glow. Yes, both for the bride-to-be and all of her new admirers, those diamonds are kept shined to perfection.

Contrast this new bride-to-be with her counterpart, say, ten years later. Now we have a much more seasoned, married woman. This woman may very likely have a young family that she's chasing around all day—possibly even in the midst of work or other pursuits. So what about that engagement ring? Hopefully it's still worn with pride, but it certainly isn't kept so shiny. This busy, seasoned, married woman has lost the original excitement over the beauty of her ring; she may be lucky to clean it once every few months—no matter how much lotion, play-dough, or cleaning supplies tarnish the glow.

As our engagement rings go, so, quite often, do our relationships (particularly the romantic ones, but even friendships or other relationship may fall into this same pattern). At first, we have all the time and energy in the world to be with and spoil our loved one. The excitement over the new, passionate relationship keeps us focused and on-track with one another. Ten years later though? Ten years later, the excitement may have faded…along with the passion that kept us focused. Now, like those diamond rings, our relationships need a little TLC more than ever to maintain their shine, yet they are less likely to get it.

As our relationships mature with time, their shine does not have to fade away; however, it takes quite a bit of intentionality for most of us to keep it in place. It's true—we must put regular time and effort into keeping our relationships healthy and on-track if we want them to keep shining. In fact, the busier we get and the more time passes, the more our relationships are likely to need this intentional effort so that they don't get squeezed out in the midst of all our other pursuits and priorities in life. Consequently, this chapter focuses on how to prioritize our relationships in order to keep that "shine"; it also highlights a number of signs that our relationships are off-track and introduces specific ways to re-introduce intentionality toward nourishing our relationships.

Practice the Pyramid

As we seek to intentionally nourish our relationships, we must first figure out how to prioritize them with all of the other things vying for our attention. There are undoubtedly as many opinions on prioritizing as there are people in the world. Nonetheless, as two psychologists, here's what we recommend: Relationships come first, before work or money. This part probably isn't too controversial…in theory at least. We'll talk more about how to practice it in a little bit. In the meantime, what about within relationships? How do we prioritize all of the various relationships we are trying to balance? Reading from the base of the pyramid up, we suggest the following:

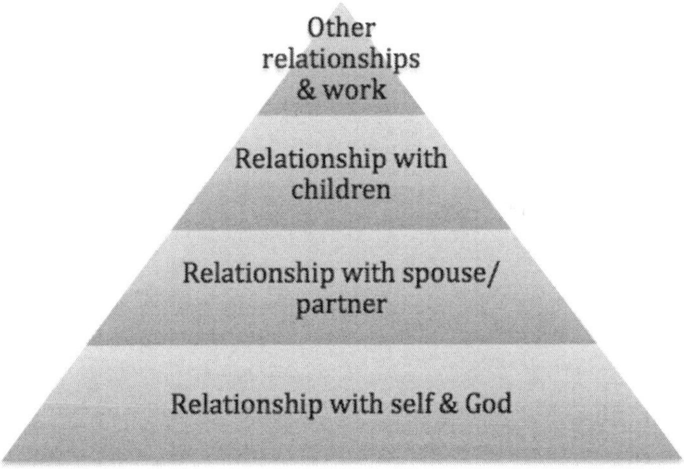

There are a few important things to point out about the chart above. First of all, relationships with God and self must come first, as the foundation to our pyramid. We sometimes want to put these relationships off, prioritizing others above ourselves. Although it's great to be generous and unselfish, we simply have nothing meaningful or good to give others if we aren't first taking care of ourselves. Yes, like everything else in life, this is a balance. Still, we must get ourselves grounded and cared for before we actually have resources to give others.

After grounding ourselves, we are wise to prioritize the relationship with our spouse—yes, even above our children! This is another piece of the pyramid that's often reversed. It's very easy to put our children above our spouse. This may be something to consider in step-families, but aside from that we must put our spouse first. Why? Because otherwise we give all of our resources to our children and have nothing left for our spouse; over time, this causes our marriages and families to deteriorate. In reality, this is not good for us or our children. Hence, we contend that, in most circumstances, our spouse or partner is prioritized second, followed closely by our children.

Notice that extended family, friends, and work all rank together in the last place on the relational pyramid. Which one comes first may depend on our season in life or our general beliefs and priorities. For example, we may have a season where we need to work hard to provide for our families, allowing us less time to spend with friends than we'd like. Although this never gives us permission to be workaholics who have no friends, it is true that our priorities may shift around within this section of the pyramid based upon our season in life. Regardless of which ranks first between family, friends, and work, though, they always come after our immediate families. Again, this is probably not too controversial…in theory. In practice, however, it's common to put our mother's feelings over our spouse's, or spend more time with our work or friends than our children. These behaviors are usually a symptom of something else, such as marital problems or boundary issues. It's important to watch for them and learn how to place our immediate families before extended family, friends, and work—both in theory and practice.

The distinction between theory and practice is an important one in applying the relational pyramid. First, it's important for each one of us to stop and figure out what we theoretically believe about the hierarchy of life. For example, does work or one's marriage come first? How about one's spouse or mother? These can be tricky questions, yet—as we've done—it behooves each one of us to take whatever time we need to answer these questions for ourselves. Once we've answered them, we hit the really tricky part: Living out our pyramid, or turning our theory in practice. This is where many of us fall short, and something we will address shortly. For now, it's important to take some time to consider whether you agree with our pyramid or would draw yours slightly differently—both in theory and practice.

Watch for Warning Signs

When we aren't applying our pyramid in practice, or otherwise nurturing our relationships, there are likely some warning signs that things are going awry. Contrary to common misconceptions, people don't simply wake up one day and "fall out of love." There is usually a long process of getting to this point. Recognizing the warning signs that a critical relationship is taking a downward spiral is an essential piece to keeping it healthy. Keep an eye out for the following:

~Repeat arguments: Most couples fight. Far from being a bad thing, this can be a sign of health that the couple is dealing with their sources of conflict. However,

when couples begin to have the same arguments over and over again about the same issues (usually things like sex, money, or in-laws), this may be a warning sign. These unresolved issues can erode the basis of the relationship, causing one party to develop disrespect for the other, and the second person very likely to withdraw. Repeat arguments are definitely a warning sign that should be addressed, even if it means getting professional help.

~*Lack of physical intimacy:* Another common warning sign is a lack of physical intimacy. Specifically, a couple may no longer connect physically. In other words, their sex life may tank. We're not talking about simply a short, busy season brought on by traveling for work or a new addition to the family; instead, this is a pattern of physical distance that lasts and grows over time. If there are sexual problems, they need to be addressed with the proper professionals (e.g., physicians, therapists). Like it or not (and thankfully most people like it!), sexuality is an integral part of our romantic relationships.

~*Lack of emotional intimacy:* Along the same lines, although much more insidious, a lack of emotional intimacy can also be a warning sign in our relationships. This basically boils down to losing the friendship with our spouse or partner. Ideally, our friendship—that is, emotional closeness, playfulness, etc.—simply builds over time. We need these aspects of a friendship to foster closeness and maintain our connection. When we instead find ourselves spending less and less time with our partners or not connecting even when we do, this is definitely a problem. Couples who want to make it for the long haul must foster this sense of friendship and emotional intimacy.

> *Dr. Puff*: "I went out to dinner with my wife recently and was shocked by our experience. Actually, we had a great time. The couple at the table next to us, however, never spoke to one another. They spent the entire dinner on their electronic devices, doing who knows what. They had almost zero eye contact or conversation. Clearly, I don't know this couple. I can definitely say that if this is a pattern, however, their relationship is in trouble."

~Relationship = partnership: As the above warning signs progress, our relationships can deteriorate to the point that they are mere partnerships. And, no, we don't mean partnerships in any good, intimate sense. We are referring here to those relationships that merely become contracts to take care of the house and kids. Although these arrangements may work for a time, they are definitely an advanced sign of relational deterioration. Far from working long-term, they are likely to lead eventually to an end to the relationship all together.

None of the signs listed above are rocket science. In fact, it'd probably be pretty obvious to us that our relationship with our child or a friend wasn't going well if we simply stopped spending time together or fought about the same things constantly. Somehow, in the busyness of life, however, we tend to miss these warning signs when it comes to our romantic relationships. The good news is that now we know and can develop a radar to detect these things as they happen. Whether it's repeat arguments, a lack of emotional or physical intimacy, or an increasing sense of mere partnership, we can now raise the warning flag and respond appropriately.

10 Ways to Shine

Whether we are responding to warning signs or simply wanting to nourish our relationships before things get problematic, there are a number of things we can do to keep the shine in our relationships. Many of these things boil down to making targeted, intentional space for our relationships to flourish. In this sense, our relationships are a lot like gardens. If we want to keep a garden looking nice, we have to schedule regular time to water, pull weeds, trim, and more. Without this time and effort, even the most beautiful garden in the world will wither and die. Similarly, our relationships require ongoing, intentional efforts to keep them flourishing. Consider these ten specific ways to maintain the vibrancy in relationships:

1) Daily check-ins: The first, and most obvious way, to keep our relationships shining is to simply spend time together, hopefully face-to-face. Daily check-ins require setting aside a specific time everyday to talk for anywhere from 5-30 minutes. This time can start with a general check in about one another's day. It may also include affirmations, apologies if either person has been hurt during the day, and possibly sharing some physical affection.

2) Weekly date nights: This idea may be as old as time, but it's still useful. Weekly date nights involve getting out together as a couple and simply enjoying one another's company. It's not time to catch up on the kids' schedule or rehash the latest argument. Instead, it's time to connect and simply build some positivity and intimacy in the relationship.

3) Quarterly retreats: Another great way to spend positive time together is through quarterly retreats. Ideally, these might be weekends away together. Realistically, even a stay-cation, or an overnight at a local hotel while the kids stay home with a babysitter, can be great. The important thing is to schedule these times and, like the weekly date-nights, make them enjoyable and connective. "Unplugging" from computers, email, and other electronic devices as much as possible can really enrich these times too.

4) Dream together: In addition to simply spending enjoyable time together, relationships flourish when they share future goals and dreams. Hence, it's great to set some time aside for dreaming together. These conversations may lead to dreams for the couple/family as well as individual dreams that one's partner can support. Ideally, the dreams can even be turned into specific goals that a couple can work toward.

5) Work together: As wonderful as it is to get time away from the daily grind together, it's also important that a couple can successfully manage the daily grind together. We suggest weekly, monthly, or even quarterly meetings to check-in about scheduling, finances, goals, or other practical aspects of the relationship. Like anything, these meetings must be scheduled and prioritized. A specific agenda listing what each person wants to cover can be helpful as well.

Dr. White: "My husband and I combine a number of these ideas through what we call our 'vision weekend.' We schedule a weekend every year to have some time away. During this weekend, we unplug completely from all electronic devices. We spend the first day simply connecting and reflecting on all the ways we've grown and been blessed in the previous year. The second day is dedicated to dreaming and eventually planning for the next year. We make sure to get very specific here, even creating a budget and other specific goals for the year to come. During the rest of the year, we have monthly meetings to review our goals and our budget. We review obstacles and are simply intentional about staying on-track with where we want to go. This process is very connective for us; it's also an intentional way to both dream together and manage the business of life in a connective way."

6) Communicate: Clearly, communication is an important key to the success of any relationship. When communicating, we recommend focusing specifically on how each person feels and what they desire in the relationship (e.g., "I feel hurt by ___, and I'd like to ask that you ____"). This formula allows us to avoid character attacks, generalizations, and other things that easily get us off-track in our conversations. Although it's outside the scope of this chapter to discuss it in detail, more information on communication can be found in Dr. White's ebook "R u red-e 4 conflict? Speaking Human in the Digital Age" (available on her website at www.kristenmwhite.com).

7) Pull weeds: Ideally, our positive communication can be used to deal with the weeds in our relationships—or those ongoing fights and problems that threaten to choke out the life we're creating. This doesn't mean that all problems are resolvable, but it does mean that we need to find a way to compromise or otherwise make peace with them. As we discussed, leaving problems as ongoing issues will create regular fights and build resentment, which can create major problems in the future.

8) Develop new skills: It's important to emphasize that many of the things we've discussed so far don't come naturally. Some of us may have difficulty with sharing intimate time (physically or emotionally), while others may have a hard time communicating and resolving problems well. When this is the case, it's critical to work on these problem areas, developing the skills we need both individually and as a couple.

9) Get help: Sometimes we can pull weeds, develop new skills, and manage other aspects of our relationships alone. Oftentimes, however, we need help. It's okay to be creative and take advantage of resources here. Read a book, meet with a spiritual leader, or go to therapy. We are particularly biased toward the last option, of course, but other steps are great too when they can help.

10) Build community: Clearly, relationships don't exist (or often work) in a vacuum. Hence, we also advocate building community to support one's relationship. It's ideal to have both individual and couple friends. Most importantly, however, our friends must be people who will honestly give us feedback during difficult times rather than simply taking our side during every argument. In this way, community can support the nourishment of our relationships as well.

In actuality, all ten of these areas can nourish our relationships. We can benefit from intentionally having fun, connective time on a daily, weekly, and quarterly basis. We can also build our relationships through dreaming and working together in the business of life. In order to do these things, we'll need to communicate well and deal with unresolved issues, even when it means developing new skills or getting help from friends or professionals. Engaging in all of these areas will help our relationships shine.

Putting It into Practice

As the list above makes clear, keeping our relationships flourishing involves intentionally working at them. We must appropriately prioritize our relationships, recognize warning signs that they may be going awry, and put regular time and effort into them. This time and effort doesn't have to be a chore. It can (and should) involve a lot of fun activities and connective time. However, this time also needs to involve dealing with ongoing issues by resolving arguments, addressing our skill deficits, getting help, and more. All of these steps will help us to nurture our relationships, keeping them as vibrant and shiny as they were when we first fell in love and exchanged rings.

So where do we start with all of this? For those who are partnered in some way, we encourage you to look through the list above and choose one way that you will intentionally nourish your relationship this week. It doesn't matter if your relationship is fantastic or strained; regardless, choose something that you are interested in doing, schedule it, and move ahead. If your partner's willing to participate, feel free to choose a joint activity, like asking them to do "daily check-ins" with you every day for the week. Again, make sure to get specific, scheduling the specific time and agenda for these check-ins everyday. In other words, your assignment is to choose a way you will nourish your relationship, create a plan, and follow through.

We do recognize that this step may be more difficult in strained relationships. When we are at odds with our partner, we tend to want to point the finger and wait for the other person to change. We understand this, but we still encourage you to try. Even if your partner isn't willing to actively participate, you can plan a nice night for him/her or even go and get help completely independently with a skill deficit of your own. We know this will be hard, and we remind you that simply being *your best* is likely to bring out the best in your partner too.

For those who are single, we encourage you to choose another relationship to nourish this week. Again, it can be one that's flourishing or struggling; simply make sure it's one that really matters to you. Once you've chosen the relationship, follow the same steps described above—choosing an activity from the list, creating a plan, and following through. You may have to make some modifications, such as creating a girls night out instead of a date night. That's okay. Even with these modifications, you are practicing being the very best relational partner that you can be, which will serve both your current relationships and any future romantic ones to come.

Questions for Reflection

1) How easy or difficult was it for me to choose an activity from the list above? Does this tell me anything about the amount of time I currently spend in nourishing my relationship(s)?

2) What obstacles did I encounter in creating and following through with my plan? What do these obstacles tell me about myself and/or the relationship?

3) What were the benefits to intentionally nourishing my relationship this week?

4) What is my personal pyramid for prioritizing relationships? Is this pyramid merely a theory, or do I practice it too?

5) Are there any warning signs in my important relationships? If so, which signs, and how will I address them using the ten ideas for making my relationship shine?

Tip #15: Just Say No!

During the 1980's and early 1990's, the US adopted "just say no" as part of their campaign against drugs. The idea was to teach kids about peer pressure and substance use, coaching them to say no in this arena. The idea seems rather simplistic, and the debate still rages about whether it worked. Regardless, we contend that the strategy, "just say no," may sometimes be powerful advice in our own lives.

Specifically, we'd like to provide this strategy for relationships. Sometimes, the best thing we can do with people is, "just say no." For example, perhaps a friend asks us to do something illegal. The answer? "Just say no." Similarly, if our boss wants us to work through our wife's birthday party, hopefully, we can again, "just say no." These scenarios, and many more like them, are all about setting boundaries with other people.

Like the anti-drug campaign, "just saying no" sounds really simple. As many of us know, however, it isn't always so easy in practice. We have to figure out when it's appropriate to say no and how to say it. Even when the time is obvious, it can be very difficult to actually muster up the courage to say it. Hence, this chapter discusses both how to be discerning in choosing our boundaries and how to express them well.

Boundaries: Why Bother?

Before we discuss how to set boundaries, it's important to address the "who cares" factor. Are boundaries really important? Can't we just go along with others and make the best of whatever situations arise? Sometimes, perhaps, we can. Very often, however, boundaries are a critical piece of protecting both ourselves and others.

First, boundaries protect us as individuals. Boundaries essentially set up fences that determine what we allow into our lives and what we do not. A very simple example of this relates to our hobbies and free time. Many people will watch “R” rated movies, but not “NC-17” rated ones (or perhaps even “PG-13” movies, but not “R”). Why? This is a boundary set up to protect these people from the sexuality or violence that is depicted in the higher rated films. This is a simple idea of a boundary that we set up to control what comes into our lives and essentially protect ourselves from unwanted influences. In fact, this is the beauty of boundaries; they set guidelines around what we allow into our lives—even in our hobbies and free time—in order to accept the influences we find beneficial and reject the ones we do not.

Similarly, boundaries can protect us within our relationships. Like the activities we choose for our hobbies and free time, some people may be a better influence on us than others; as a result, we may choose to set boundaries about how much time or closeness we have with more negative or critical people, for example. At the same time, even really wonderful people will sometimes ask more of us than we can give, and boundaries allow us to say no, protecting our time, resources, etc. For example, perhaps our friend asks us to babysit her children. If we need that time to study for a test or run our weekly errands, an answer of "no" sets up a boundary that clearly communicates what we are capable of giving within the relationship. Whether boundaries are used with friends, co-workers, family, or others, they state clearly what we will allow in and what we can give out.

In addition to clearly communicating about and protecting ourselves, boundaries also protect our relationships. Just as we say, "no" to things that would impede too much upon our resources or time, we can similarly say, "no" to things that would impede upon our relationships. For example, perhaps we turn down the friend's request to babysit, or our mother's desire to come over, in order to protect the time and connection we have with our own spouse or children. Again, these boundaries protect what's most important to us, allowing us to make our theoretical priorities a reality.

Some people view boundaries as selfish. We'd like to dispel that myth here. It's not selfish to protect oneself and one's relationships—it's wise. We are silly to think we can give all things, to all people, at all times. We are also unrealistic to believe that we can always meet everyone's needs or desires for us and our time. Trying to live up to this type of expectation is crazy-making and costly to both ourselves and our relationships. Living within our actual means allows us to give joyously and fully when we give.

Dr. White: "I definitely used to believe that setting boundaries was selfish. On some level, I thought that

I existed to simply give to others; as a result, I was convinced that the most godly thing I could do was give unendingly, regardless of any consequences. Over time, I learned this was unrealistic and crazy. When I give past my means, I give out of exhaustion and duty; when I give out of my abundance because I'm caring for myself, I give out of love and desire. And, I believe, the latter produces much better results—both for me and for those receiving! I now look at setting boundaries as a gift. I am clearly communicating what I can give and what I can't. I utterly appreciate it when others do the same for themselves. If they do not communicate clearly, I am left trying to read their minds and interpret what they actually have to give, which is a job that I don't want. I understand firsthand why boundaries can be construed as selfish, but I really experience them as honest and caring in a way that ignoring our limits or needs is not."

As Dr. White illustrates, setting boundaries can actually be a gift to both ourselves and others. In setting boundaries, we protect ourselves and our relationships from things we either do not want or simply do not have the resources to accept. At the same time, we give the gift of honest communication to the other party. We do not force them to guess at what we are really thinking, but instead we communicate clearly. In this way, setting boundaries actually protects more than just ourselves—it also protects the other party. Hence, boundaries are a gift of clarity and honesty to both ourselves and others.

Choosing the Line

So we need boundaries, but where do we possibly begin in figuring out where they should go? Where do we draw the lines about what we will accept in or not? Good news! We've already gotten a head start on this. In the last chapter, we talked about and looked at our own priorities. We examined how relationships rank in comparison to one another as well as in relation to other tasks in our lives, like work. This pyramid is the best place to start in setting our boundaries.

For example, imagine that our in-laws ask to come and stay with us after the birth of our new baby. How do we begin to decide whether we are okay with this, or whether we need to set a boundary? First, we consult our pyramid. Our in-laws probably rank below ourselves, our spouse, and our new child. So, will having them around enhance these relationships or tax them? There is no right answer to this question, as it may vary for each one of us. The goal, however, is that we put our priorities into actual practice, using our pyramid to help guide us.

There are two important things to note about the example above. First, it's not necessarily black and white. We might decide that our family can enjoy a little time with the in-laws but would be taxed by having them around for weeks on end. As a result, perhaps we invite the in-laws to stay for a limited number of days. The point? Boundaries don't have to be all-or-nothing. They can be flexible to work for us and others.

At the same time, boundaries require discernment. Specifically, we must be able to assess the impact something may have upon us and our relationships. Again, this applies to everything from relationships to our hobbies. Does time with our friend encourage us, or pull us into a negative spiral? Does watching the evening news or those new, Blockbuster movies make us aspire to be better people or leave us feeling depressed? Does keeping on top of email all day via our Smartphone make us feel on top of things or scattered? Making choices and setting boundaries requires us to be honest and discerning about how things really impact us. We all have different sensitivities here, which may even vary during different seasons in our lives, so there are no right or wrong answers. The important thing is to act on what's honoring of ourselves and the things that matter most in our lives.

Dr. Puff: "Many years ago, I began to recognize that watching most TV shows is not uplifting for me. I began seeing that the images and words from the shows stuck with me. It actually hit me when I heard some loud music on my way to a camping trip and had it running through my head for two full days! It turns out that the things we hear and see really matter, even if it is largely at a subconscious level. As a result, I'm very discerning in what I listen to and watch. I make sure that the things surrounding me and going into my mind are uplifting. In terms of TV, this means I don't watch much; when I do watch, it tends to be PG movies with the kids or esoteric DVDs about things like monks and enlightenment. Sticking to this boundary is pretty easy now, but it was not without its challenges at first. It sometimes involved picking the harder way of finding something else to do, even when I was with someone who really wanted to watch a movie or TV show I didn't like. For me, though, the boundary is worth it because it allows my mind to be filled with positive and uplifting messages and images."

Dr. Puff's story illustrates how we can set boundaries about what we choose to allow into our lives and not—both in and out of relationships. Hopefully, we use our priorities and some old-fashioned discernment to choose what those things are for us. Then we act on them, having the courage we need to say "no" in the appropriate places. There are a lot of areas for us to consider setting boundaries, but the principles of priorities and discernment are similar across all settings.

Drawing the Line

Once we establish where to set boundaries, things get really tricky: The next step is to actually make them known. It can take a lot of courage to set boundaries, as they aren't always popular with those around us. In fact, boundaries tend to be particularly unpopular when our friends and family aren't used to us setting them. So how do we begin in drawing the line? Consider the following tips:

~Be clear and direct: Clarity and directness are the most important components to setting boundaries. Rather than beating around the bush, it's critical to state

our boundaries in straightforward, simple language. Being ambiguous lends itself to questions, argument, and confusion. In contrast, being clear is more likely to be heard, understood, and perhaps even respected. As we are clear and direct, it's also important to be very specific in what we want. For example, let's say that we have decided our in-laws can stay with us for only two nights on their trip out. Rather than stating something ambiguous like, "You know, we'd love to have you…we're just not sure if it will work…we're concerned about space and schedules…" we might state clearly, "We look forward to seeing you. Due to our personal constraints, we can only host you at the house for one or two nights. If you'd like to stay longer than that, we'd be happy to help you find a hotel." This second statement is specific, clear, and direct—leaving much less room for confusion or negotiation.

~Be kind, but don't apologize: As we are expressing our boundaries to others, it's possible to be very kind without being overly apologetic. The example above illustrates this well. We start out positive by stating that we do look forward to having our in-laws visit. We then clearly state our boundaries—without apologizing. We all have limits and it's truly okay to express them to others. We can be warm and genuine without bending over backward to "make it up to them" or otherwise apologize profusely. Again, this latter type of behavior—apologizing profusely—is more likely to garner arguments from the other party. It also leaves us holding a lot of unnecessary guilt. Hence, we aim to be

caring and compassionate without carrying the responsibility for pleasing the entire world all the time.

~Be reasonable, but firm: When setting boundaries, it's also critical to be reasonable yet firm. Ideally, we decide specifically what our boundaries are in advance. It's fine to take the other party into account and choose something as honoring and reasonable for both sides as possible. Once we decide on the boundary, however, it's essential that we are firm. Firmness is important because it's really true that if we give an inch, the other party may take a mile. This adage is especially true if we are setting boundaries for the first time in relationships. Once we draw the line, the other party will come to respect it much more quickly if we are firm. Part of being firm is also following through and being consistent. If we communicate a boundary and then let it slide, the other party is much more likely to push and doubt our boundaries in the future. Hence, our goal is to set reasonable boundaries and then be firm and consistent in keeping them.

~Walk away if needed: It's very possible that the other party may not like our boundaries. That's okay. We don't necessarily owe any explanation, although it is okay to try and give one if the other party is asking. Realistically, however, this may or may not be effective. If the other party continues to push, argue, or even ridicule us or our boundary, it's time to simply walk away (even if the other party doesn't like this). Continuing to argue will get us nowhere…except perhaps in an increasingly heated, emotional conversation in which

either person may say things he/she regrets. Hence, we sometimes need to agree to disagree, trusting in the boundary we thoughtfully set in advance. At times, this may mean walking away without full resolution, hopefully repairing the relationship in some way at a later time when both parties are calmer.

When boundaries are new, they can seem very confusing, scary, and overwhelming. We don't know where to start or what to say. We are afraid of how the other person will react. Sometimes things go way better than we expect…and occasionally they are as bad, or even worse, than we feared. The good news is that it gets much easier with time. We learn to be specific, clear, warm, and direct while also being firm, consistent, and unapologetic. Overall, we get better at setting boundaries, and those around us come to expect them from us and respect them more.

Putting It into Practice

Boundaries can be a pretty controversial topic. Many people experience this kind of self-assertion as selfish, confusing, or overwhelming. Although we recognize the challenge inherent in setting boundaries, we believe that doing so is actually quite wise and helpful for both ourselves and others. More specifically, boundaries allow us to protect ourselves and our relationships by recognizing our limits and stating clearly what we can joyfully give and receive in our lives. Boundaries also allow a clear line of communication that can be helpful to both parties. Hence, boundaries are actually a wise, compassionate, clear way to live and interact.

So how do we institute boundaries in our own lives? First, we are discerning about where to set them. We consider our priorities and how specific people or activities impact us. We can be flexible, but we are also completely honest. Once we figure out where to set boundaries, then we try to be clear, direct, and specific in communicating them. We are reasonable and kind without being overly apologetic or too flexible. Hopefully, the other party respects our boundaries; when they don't, however, we may explain briefly and then agree to disagree, trusting in the thoughtful work we did to choose the boundary in the first place. Although challenging at first, this process gets much easier with time—both on ourselves and on others, as we know how to engage it and they come to expect and respect it. Soon, we can be, "just saying no" like the pros!

To start setting boundaries in your own life, we recommend that you take some time to think through where they may be needed. Where are you giving out of duty and obligation instead of love and joy? What activities or relationships bring you down instead of up? What activities or relationships reverse the priorities in your pyramid? Keep in mind that your answer to these questions may reveal places where you need new boundaries (or simply firmer ones) in relationships, hobbies, work, or more. Take some time to think through these questions and choose at least one place in your life that you need to set a new boundary.

Next, spend some time thinking through what a healthy boundary would look like in this area or relationship. Be honest with yourself as you discern the impact of this area on your life and relationships. Consider journaling or discussing it with a trusted friend or counselor. Try to separate guilt and "should's" from what is really possible and life-giving for you. Feel free to take a few days to think through your boundary; there is no need to rush this decision.

Once you've chosen your boundary, you've arrived at the really tricky party—expressing it. Here, again, we'd like you to take your time. Consider who you need to share you boundary with, and then take time to practice. You may find it helpful to write out a sample script of how to express yourself directly, clearly, warmly, and unapologetically. Then practice it in the car or in front of the mirror. If possible, even ask a friend or loved one to role play the scenario with you. If you expect to get some push back on your boundary, ask them to play this part and practice responding. When you feel confident in what you need to say, then you are ready: Go communicate your boundary. As always, return and answer the questions for reflection when you're done.

Questions for Reflection

1) How easy or hard was it for me to figure out where I need additional boundaries in my life? Does this tell me anything about how much or how little I currently set boundaries?

2) Did I notice any themes around where I need additional boundaries (e.g., specific relationships, hobbies, etc.)?

3) How easy or difficult was it for me to figure out how to communicate my chosen boundary? Is communicating boundaries an area I feel confident in, or one that could use some extra work?

4) How did it go when I actually expressed the boundary? What did I do well? Also, was there anything I could improve upon next time (e.g., being more direct, apologizing less)?

5) What are my next steps in working on boundaries in my own life?

Tying It All Together

Relationships are a critical and amazing part of life. They both impact us and allow us to impact others. Because of their strong influence and huge place in our lives, it's essential that we are intentional about relationships in our lives. First, we make efforts to form good ones that will have a positive impact on us and enrich our lives. In order to do this, we not only need to find positive, like-minded, healthy people—we also need to *be* positive, healthy people. By simply paying attention to these two factors of finding and being the best people possible, we can join the greatest athletes in the world in *forming a good team.*

Once we form these awesome teams or relationships, we also need to be intentional about maintaining them. Like just about anything in life that we value, relationships require maintenance. The good news, however, is that these efforts don't have to be a chore. Yes, we need to be attentive to any negative warning signs that our relationships are going awry, and we need to deal with ongoing issues. Nonetheless, relationships that spend time on regular maintenance usually involve a lot of fun, connective activities which easily nurture them into flourishing. In both these little and big as well as difficult and pleasurable ways, we can *keep our relationship diamonds shiny*—just like the first days when we fell in love.

An important part of maintaining our relationships and keeping them shiny is also protecting them. We do this through boundaries. Although boundaries are challenging for many people, they are actually a gift to us that allows us to protect both ourselves and our relationships. They also encourage clear communication that can be beneficial to both the person giving and receiving the boundary. There are a number of steps we can take to begin instituting boundaries in our lives, including being wise about where they are needed and being clear, direct, and specific in communicating them. Although it may take practice, setting boundaries is a healthy step that can allow us to "*just say no*" at the most appropriate times and places.

Although relationships can feel complicated to a lot of people, we contend that these three steps will get them on-track. First, form good relationships by being and finding healthy, positive people. Second, maintain these relationships by both attending to trouble and just intentionally connecting and having fun. Third, protect them from any outside influences that would cause deterioration by setting wise, clear boundaries. In one sense these are three simple steps; in another, they are three steps that we could spend a lifetime learning. Still, they are the three steps that will get us moving more and more in sync with our partners, dancing with increasing skill, ease, and grace.

Part VI: Work & Finances

We've looked at many different parts of the dance, ranging from being in sync with one's partner(s) to having solid mental focus. But what about simply having the skill to perform the movements? This piece may not be super important for the carefree child, but it is extremely critical for the skilled master. The master must have a certain amount of solid skill in order to dance well.

And how does the master learn this skill? Hard work. Yep, we said it. In some ways, we've actually been saying it over and over throughout this book—to be good at dancing or anything else in life, we have to learn the skills and practice them. No matter how you slice it, life entails some of this work.

At the same time, we don't believe that this work has to be painstaking and unpleasant. In fact, for the professional dancer, it's pretty critical that this is not the case. Yes, every professional may endure some pain, but if the practice isn't also enjoyable on some level, the dancer is going to lose heart. And, no, it's not enough to just enjoy one aspect of the dance, like the performances. The professional dancer must find some ways to enjoy the work of practicing and learning skills too.

In life, this translates to us finding ways to enjoy the work of life. This work may sometimes be learning new skills, like those contained in this book. Most of the time, though, it's the day-in and day-out tasks of life, including everything from engaging in our careers to taking care of our families to managing our money. Like the dancer, we must find ways to enjoy these activities, even in the midst of the work we are putting into them. And, again like the dancer, it isn't enough to simply wait and enjoy the result or the weekend; we will miss out on too much of life and perhaps even lose heart if that is the case.

As a result, this section focuses on how to manage our work and finances. We'll focus specifically on how to enjoy and thrive in our careers first. Please note, however, that many of these same tips can be applied to other "work," like taking care of the kids and managing one's home. We'll also devote an entire chapter to money because we know this can be an empowering or sabotaging influence in our lives all by itself. Although we don't have the space to be exhaustive, our goal is to help infuse some life and pleasure into these areas so that they can go from energy-killers and time-suckers to things that increase our ability to thrive holistically—just like those professional dancers who get to do what they love for a living.

Tip #16: Follow the Pleasure Principle

The "pleasure principle" is a psychological idea that's at least as old as Freud himself. It postulates that we are motivated to do certain things and not others out of the desire to maximize pleasure and avoid pain. Sound simple? It certainly is. Even Freud recognized this, simultaneously theorizing that, as we grow up, we are increasingly motivated by the "reality principle," which allows us to defer pleasure or gratification for greater, longer-term gains. In other words, we learn over time to put off pleasure now so that we can get more of it later (e.g., saving our money today so that we can buy a bigger toy tomorrow).

There is a lot of wisdom in this deferral of gratification, yet it can sometimes be overdone. Specifically, we sometimes treat our professional life too much as a painful, hard-core reality instead of one of pleasure. Yes, it's true: We do need to work in order to make money to put food on the table and otherwise provide for ourselves and our families. There is indeed a very poignant truth behind following the reality principle in work. However, this truth does not necessarily have to be all-or-nothing or incredibly painful.

We can actually enjoy our work too. Although we tend to treat work as a "must" instead of a desire, it is possible to make it something we enjoy on a day-to-day basis. It is possible to make it a source of pleasure. In fact, we contend that we are more likely to find both satisfaction and success when we make work as much a source of pleasure as something which meets real needs. In this chapter, we'll discuss why this is the case and how to make it happen in our lives.

Head Toward Satisfaction & Success

We'd probably all love to enjoy our work. We can easily see how much time we spend there in a given day or week, and we realize pretty quickly that it would be great to enjoy it. But does it really matter? Can't we just hunker down and endure the grind day after day? Sadly, to a large degree, we probably can. We may get by with just dragging ourselves through the grind. We certainly don't recommend this strategy though. We recommend finding (or creating) a work that we really love.

When we have work that we enjoy (at least most of the time), we are much more likely to find a sense of *satisfaction.* First, we gain satisfaction at work. When we enjoy our jobs, we are more likely to walk through the day with a positive attitude; we also tend to come home with a sense of accomplishment and perhaps even joy. And what happens then? Surprise, surprise, we also suddenly find more satisfaction in our families, hobbies, finances, and all of the other things waiting for us at home. Why? Because we are ending the day or week with a positive outlook. We end up wearing a rosier colored pair of glasses, which provide a better outlook for the other things in our lives too. Simply imagine the man who comes home from work grumpy because of a boring, conflict-filled day versus the one who comes home invigorated by the tasks and meaning of the day; it's easy to see which one is more likely to enjoy his family and other activities. Clearly, enjoying our work can increase our satisfaction with both our professional and our personal lives.

Interestingly, enjoying our work is also likely to increase our *success* in life. No matter how disciplined we are, we put more effort into the things that we actually enjoy. We feel more passion for these things and we naturally gravitate toward wanting to learn and do more with them. Simply imagine the woman who hates, let's say, being a teacher versus the one who loves it; the first woman is likely to do a mediocre job as she tries to get out of the classroom as quickly as possible, while the second woman may very well put her heart and soul into perfecting lesson plans, designing a stimulating classroom, and even learning more about how to teach well. The passion of the person who loves her work leads her to put in more effort, which eventually leads to greater mastery and even excellence in the field. And what happens then? Success! That's right, having a job we enjoy leads to greater success as well as satisfaction.

Hopefully it's clear, then, why it matters that we find a job we enjoy. It's not just a "nice to have," or a perk, in life. Having a job we enjoy actually sets us up to have greater success and satisfaction in our careers. And, that, in turn, sets us up to have greater satisfaction (and perhaps even success) in life. This is why we don't recommend simply dragging ourselves through the grind day after day; it's not just unpleasant to do this, it may actually be costly. Instead, it makes a lot more sense to follow the pleasure principle into work we can enjoy.

Seek Your Love

For some people, the work they enjoy may be obvious. Either they are already doing it, or they've clearly known all along what it is they'd love to do, and they just need to take a few risks to move toward it. For others, it may be a little harder to figure out what would be enjoyable professionally. For these latter groups, here are a few tips for getting started on figuring out what work we could love and beginning to walk down this path:

-Focus on what's energizing: The best place to start in figuring out work we could enjoy is paying attention to what we already enjoy in life. What are the activities that leave us feeling energized and invigorated? And what circumstances (e.g., with people vs. alone, inside vs. outside, morning vs. evening) add to or detract from these feelings? If the answers to these questions aren't immediately clear, it may help to start keeping a journal during the day, noticing one's energy level during and after each activity. Sometimes career aptitude tests can help here too. Either way, it's important to find patterns of activities and circumstances that energize us.

-Pay attention to what provides meaning: Similarly, the things that provide us meaning in life can create enjoyment on another level. What causes, principles, etc. are we passionate about? Where do we derive a sense of meaning beyond ourselves in life? These questions may take us back to our spirituality or in

another direction entirely. Either way, enfolding deep meaning into our work is another way to garner a deep sense of accomplishment, satisfaction, and enjoyment out of it.

Dr. White: "If I'm honest, I had no idea what I wanted to do after I finished college. I knew I enjoyed people, so I went to work in the human resources section of the corporate world. I was very good at it, and I appreciate the opportunities I had. Unfortunately, I just didn't enjoy it on a day-to-day basis. After a lot of soul-searching, I realized that I was energized by having deep, authentic connections with friends and others on a one-on-one basis—not working on spreadsheets and answering phone calls about commission checks. What's more, I find a lot of spiritual meaning in being a part of an individual's growth and healing process. As a result, being a psychologist fits me perfectly. There are still days and moments that it's hard and I even wonder if I'm crazy for choosing to sit with people in the midst of their pain; through it all, however, I can reconnect with myself and the things that create meaning for me—all of which causes me to not only enjoy what I do, but actually to feel immensely honored and blessed to be a part of it."

~Get specific and creative: Once we figure out what provides energy and meaning to us, it's time to figure out how to turn it into a career. There are two

things to keep in mind here. First off, it's important to be very specific about what is providing us meaning and energy. For Dr. White, it wasn't enough to know she enjoyed people; she had to get much more specific in realizing that she enjoyed being with people in a deep, authentic way on a more individual basis. At the same time, we often have to get creative in how to make these specific desires a job. Dr. White was initially blind to how she could turn an enjoyment of deep connection with friends into a job, yet even this was possible! It may take some creativity, but in this day in age, it's truly possible to turn just about anything into a job or business.

~Interview experts: As we are narrowing down what we'd really like to do, it's a good idea to interview experts. If we think we might enjoy being a teacher, find people who are teachers and talk to them about their job. What does a typical day look like? What are the pros and cons, in their opinion, about being in the field? What do they wish they would have known when they started on their career path? All of these questions, and more, can help us get a good idea of whether we might actually enjoy our theoretical job in reality. At the same time, these experts can help us think outside of the box and get creative when needed. For example, is it possible to be a teacher to smaller classes or on a part-time basis? Experts can definitely help in the process of getting specific and creative in finding careers we'd enjoy.

~Weigh the pros and cons: After we talk to these experts, it's important to weigh all of the pros and cons. What education and hours are required? Do we get to

work in circumstances we enjoy? What are the financial risks and benefits? How would the job impact our other priorities in life? The list could go on and on! The important thing is to continue being specific here, and to try and find a way to make one's desires a reality. This probably means that someone who wants to be a full- or part-time, stay-at-home mom is not going to be a very good fit as a medical doctor...even if she loves the field. Hopefully, though, she wouldn't give up on this love; instead, she might find some way to work in a related capacity that allows her to connect to her desires and enjoy her work. The bottom line here is to weigh the pros and cons, and try to find a way to make our work something we can enjoy on all levels, even as it integrates with other things that are important to us in life.

All of the steps above are aimed at doing exactly that: Finding a way to make our work something we can enjoy on all levels, even as it integrates with other things that are important to us in life. This doesn't mean that our career has to be easy or fun all the time, but hopefully it will feel immensely positive overall. Eventually, walking down this path of making our job something we enjoy may take some risks or sacrifices. We may have to turn down a promotion or a higher paying job that takes us in the wrong direction. We may be challenged to start a new career at 40 or 50. It's definitely okay to take these steps slowly, minimizing risk without being paralyzed by it. Most people find that the journey pays off in the end, creating something that they enjoy immensely, excel at, and are paid enough (or sometimes even abundantly) to make life flourish in all areas.

Know When to Sweat the Small Stuff

As we are establishing a career we love, we'd also like to emphasize the importance of "the small stuff." We talked about this a little bit when we discussed the body and stress. The small stuff—from our schedules to our environment to our co-workers—really matters. Even if we are years away from having the career we truly want, we can do a lot to make our job something we enjoy now by taking control over these little things.

That's right—we generally have a lot of control over "the small stuff." Sometimes it's hard to acknowledge this. Our work gets frustrating and, quite frankly, it's easier to complain about the circumstances than do something to change or make the best of them. Most of us have been there at some time or another, so we get it. Unfortunately, we also get that bemoaning our circumstances takes us nowhere. And, like it or not, we usually have more control over the little things than we initially acknowledge.

As a result, it's time to start sweating a lot of the small stuff. This involves paying attention to how our work environment impacts us and adjusting little things to make it better. As we discussed earlier, perhaps we schedule breaks during the day to simply take a breather or do something we'd enjoy (e.g., a short walk or lunch with a friend). Maybe we put up some pictures or play some soft music that would energize us. Perhaps we even talk to our boss or co-workers about some of the things that are bothering us, requesting an adjustment in our hours, responsibilities, etc. If we do this respectfully, the worst that happens is we receive an answer of "no"...but at least we know we've tried. The process is essentially the same here as we discussed earlier in the chapter: We are finding and capitalizing on the things that energize us—we are simply doing it with the small stuff as well as the big stuff.

While we are capitalizing on and sweating the small stuff, we also have to know when to let go. Sometimes we can't control things, and the best we can do is let go and move on to things we can control. Perhaps it's impossible to make our job something we enjoy, and it's time to let go and move on to something (or someplace) we can enjoy. Maybe this is a complete career change, or maybe it's just working for a company or a staff we connect with more. Alternatively, perhaps we enjoy our job, but we just can't get everything done. Even too much of a good thing is still too much, so this too requires letting go. Whatever the circumstances, the point is to know when we've reached our limits and move on gracefully.

Dr. Puff: "I love what I do, and I'm careful (as I discussed earlier) to sweat the small stuff in taking breaks, making my work environment fit me, and more. All of this helps me to thrive. At the same time, I have to know when to let go. For me, this particularly manifests in letting go of opportunities. I frequently get calls for last minute, high-exposure interviews that I have to turn down because they'd simply add too much to my day and schedule, taking me away from the things that matter to me most (like my family). Recently, I also had to cut down significantly on the number of podcasts I'm recording because my days are too busy with seeing clients. Some people might bemoan this change, trying to hold onto and do everything. Instead, I feel blessed for the opportunities and try to let go gracefully—knowing this is not small stuff worth sweating."

As Dr. Puff's story illustrates, part of enjoying our work is knowing when to sweat the small stuff. We pay attention to the little things, like schedule and environment, that make our work day more positive. We control these things when we can…and then we let go when we can't. Sometimes the letting go allows us to take ahold of new opportunities and other things that matter. Whether it's time to sweat them or let go, all of these little things can contribute to making our job something we enjoy rather than a place we dread.

Putting It into Practice

The facts are quite simple here: We are more likely to flourish—finding satisfaction and success—in our careers and in our lives when we have work that we enjoy. What's more, the ability to flourish in both little ways and big ways is usually more in our control than we think. We don't have to simply endure 40+ hours of our week, waiting for the weekend to arrive. Yes, reality requires that we work to provide for our needs and pay for our bills. At the same time, however, our work can be a source of pleasure too; in this case, the reality principle and pleasure principle do not have to be mutually exclusive.

There are two main ways to follow the pleasure principle into creating a career that we enjoy. First, we can find work that provides us satisfaction in and of itself through the sense of meaning and energy it gives us. Second, we can pay attention to the little details of our career, like scheduling and environment, which make our days significantly more or less positive. With these details, we learn to break a sweat in controlling the ones we can and simultaneously letting go of the ones we can't. In these ways, both little and big, our work can be a source of pleasure and joy as well as income.

To begin making your work a greater source of pleasure, complete the assessment below, comparing your ideal and actual work environments. As Dr. White has modeled in her sample, get as specific as possible with the details of your actual and ideal work environments. Feel free to take your time and put in some serious thought into painting a picture of your ideal. Get creative and perhaps even talk it over with others who know you well. The sky's the limit here! After you've completed the chart, answer the questions for reflection to figure out where to go next with this activity.

	Dr. White's Sample	Your Actual	Your Ideal
Type of work	*Psychology*		
Specific activities	*Teaching, supervising, therapy, writing, speaking*		
Total hours per week	*20-30 hrs/wk*		
Daily and/or weekly schedule	*3-4 days/wk; mostly afternoons & evenings, with 5-10 min breaks every hour or two*		
Co-workers	*Few co-workers; close relationships professionally and personally*		
Location and/or Commute	*Part in N. OC office; part at home office*		
Environment	*Small office; furnished with warm paintings & comfy couches; near park for lunch walks*		
Type of business & relationship to it	*Employee of clinical psychology graduate program, and owner of small business*		

	Dr. White's Sample	Your Actual	Your Ideal
Income	*$1 million/yr (J/K!)* ☺		
Benefits	*Maternity leave and a flexible schedule needed, but no health benefits required*		
Need for Professional Development	*1-2 days/year plus keeping up on research in between*		
Other Considerations	*Hours working around childcare*		

Questions for Reflection

1) How easy or difficult was it for me to paint a picture of my ideal work environment? What does this tell me about whether I've prioritized the reality or pleasure principle in my work?

2) How does my ideal work environment compare to my actual work environment? What are the biggest points of similarity and difference?

3) Looking at the chart above, what are the three most important components to me of my ideal work environment (e.g., type of work, total hours, and childcare consideration)? *(Be honest here—answers will differ and there are no right or wrong ones!)*

4) How close is my actual work environment to the ideal in these three specific areas?

5) What next steps can I take to bring my actual work environment in line with my ideal in these three areas?

Tip #17: Get in the Zone

Beings "in the zone" is an extraordinary experience. And, no, we aren't talking about some special diet or "zoning out" in front of the TV. Being "in the zone" is, for example, when the underdog on a T.V. talent show comes to the stage for the last round with a different air about them—a strange, elevated confidence––and gives a winning performance that astounds the audience. Or, when a world-class athlete is in peak performance—undistracted and flowing with absolute clarity and confidence toward undeniable victory. These are examples of being "in the zone."

The "zone" is all about being at our peak state of performance. It's a place marked by excellence. It's when we have those moments of feeling like the ideas flow, the product comes easily, or everything falls into place. We've all experienced moments like this, and most of us wish we could recreate them. Why? Because "the zone" is an awesome place where we feel confident, engaged, and productive.

While most of us would love to experience "the zone" on a more frequent basis, we often feel like it is something that just sort-of happens. We occasionally have a great day where everything just works, but we have no idea know why. The good news is that we can intentionally create this type of experience. In other words, we can help ourselves to get into the zone and stay there on purpose. This chapter will talk about what creates "the zone," how it benefits us, and how to create it on purpose.

Understanding "the zone"

We've said that "the zone" is an awesome place where we feel confident, engaged, and positive. But why? What is unique about those moments that create this experience? The answer to this question actually goes back to other things we've already talked about in this book. Being in "the zone" is all about having a quiet mind. It is a mind that is free of unending critiques and self-talk. It is a mind that is free to simply engage in all it can do now, instead of what it experienced yesterday or might experience tomorrow. "The zone" mind is fully engaged in the present moment.

Think, for a moment, of a great performer. Perhaps we've admired the art of certain dancers, like Fred Astaire, or perhaps we've seen a Cirque du Soleil show and marveled at the acrobats. When these dancers and acrobats perform their routines, they are moving fluidly and seamlessly. They do things that make us stare in amazement at what the human body can achieve. How? Well, during these shows, the performers are not thinking about how to move their hips or get their body to tap, bend, or spin as they are executing a move. They are not concerned about whether they can pull off a move or evaluating it immediately afterwards. No, these masters are not engaging in mind-chatter. Instead, they are in the zone—completely and totally engaged in their performance.

This simple ingredient—presence—is what allows us to be in "the zone." The energy it requires to critique, question and continuously direct oneself detracts from the energy available for the activity or performance itself. As a result, performers of a high caliber train in advance so that their skill becomes second nature. Then they can simply get on stage and do it...without having to think about it. Sure, the performers may run over their routines in advance or review them after the show; during the moment of the performance, however, all thinking stops. In that moment, they simply let it flow.

It's the same with top athletes or performers in any field. Whether we are talking about the best basketball players in the world or the top CEO's, the principle is the same: They learn their craft well, and then they train themselves to go out and simply do it. Although they may call it by a variety of names, they basically use mindfulness to quiet the mind-chatter in their brains and simply be present in their craft. This combination of preparation and excellence with in-the-moment presence creates the amazing results we see from those who are in "the zone."

Benefiting from "the zone"

In fact, we can expect some incredible results and benefits from the clear mind that comes with being in "the zone." First of all, cultivating our ability to be in "the zone" can create immense *focus and confidence.* Imagine walking into the office and sitting down at the computer or standing up at a team meeting, *without* all the usual mind-chatter. Imagine that the mind is not distracted by office politics from yesterday, potential promotions tomorrow, or anything going on at home. What if we could walk into our office, retail store, or other place of business, simply knowing that we are the best we can be? In truth, this is what cultivating our ability to drop into "the zone" can do for us—it can create immense focus and confidence as we are able to simply be present and engaged in our current task.

Not surprisingly, with this focus and confidence also comes improved *productivity and results.* This improvement in our productivity and results has two parts. First, we are able to get more done when we are focused. In other words, we are more productive because we aren't distracted by the past, future, or anything else. Second, what we get done tends to be a higher quality. We not only do more when we are in "the zone," we also do it better. We write our best marketing plans, shoot the most baskets, and make the most money. That's right—being in "the zone" improves our results by increasing both the quantity and quality of our work.

Dr. White: "In many ways, becoming a therapist was all about learning to be in 'the zone.' We had to learn a number of theories and skills to work with people and help them change. However, somehow we also had to figure out how to be fully present—cognitively, emotionally, even somatically—with another person. We couldn't sit down with someone and be thinking about how all their words fit our theories or steps; if we did, we'd miss them and their story. Instead, we had to learn the skills and theories so well that they became engrained or second-nature. Then we could just go into the room and simply *be* with someone in a therapeutic way. We could let it flow naturally through us with an immense amount of focus, and achieve a great amount of results simply by being with the other person. I don't think this is the strategy every school uses to train therapists, but it is one of the reasons I appreciate my program so much. They taught us to *be* therapists rather than simply *do* therapy—a distinction that allows us to be in 'the zone' and thus experience focus, skill, results, and satisfaction in a job well done."

As Dr. White's story begins to hit upon, the increase in focus, confidence, productivity, and results that comes with being in "the zone" has *personal benefits* as well. We are less stressed and more able to enjoy our jobs. What's more, as we've touched upon time and again in this book, decreasing our stress and increasing our pleasure with work makes us enjoy our lives more in general. We're more capable of going home and enjoying our friends, family, and hobbies because we have a sense of satisfaction from a job well done instead of a sense of stress from a job still to be done. Overall, then, "the zone" is a pretty incredible place to be, providing us numerous benefits both on the job and in our personal lives.

Finding "the zone"

So how do we cultivate our ability to be in "the zone"? There are a number of things we can do to both prepare and engage in this place. Consider the following:

1) Prepare the mind: First of all, truly being in "the zone" requires a certain level of presence. We must be able to focus on our task at any given moment, setting aside what happened this morning and what we need to do later in the day. Sound familiar? We hope so! Being in "the zone" requires a certain amount of mindfulness—something we talked about earlier in this book related to the mind. In the same way we use meditation and other activities to train the mind to be present with life, we can use these things to train the mind to be present with work. In both cases, we are simply strengthening our ability to be still and present, thereby preparing our minds to be in "the zone."

2) Build the skills: It's probably pretty obvious that it's not enough to simply be present. This is a very good start, but being in "the zone" also requires that we can perform with excellence when the time comes. How do we prepare for that? We learn and practice quite diligently. We become knowledgeable about our fields and excellent in our tasks; then, like those professional athletes or CEOs, we can simply engage without having to think about what to do when the time comes. Hence, the second part of preparing to be in "the zone" is building our skills so that the performance is second-nature when the time comes.

3) Eliminate the judge: Once we have prepared both our minds and our skills, we are ready to drop into "the zone." Our greatest enemy here will be our self-critiques. As we talked about earlier, it's great to evaluate our performances at some point. However, it is not helpful to engage in that evaluation during the actual task or performance. At that moment, we must allow ourselves to be fully engaged and present, including turning off the internal, self-critic. Part of turning this off is simply preparing our minds for presence. Another part is letting go of the results in the moment. We must trust that we are fully prepared and at our best, letting the chips fall where they may.

Dr. Puff: "I experience being in 'the zone' all the time with my work. It may be best illustrated by public speaking. Speaking is a skill I've intentionally cultivated over time. I spend about 30 minutes every day, 5 days per week learning about and practicing speaking. I also spend additional time studying and engaging with the actual topics I speak on (e.g., meditation). All of this time goes into preparing my skills for the actual presentations. When they arrive, however, I just dive in. I don't read a pre-written lecture. Heck, I don't even use notes. I just allow myself to speak from my heart, knowing that I'm fully prepared and that my message will come out effortlessly. In other words, I'm able to share what I'm passionate about and trust that I am at my best because I'm fully prepared and completely engaged.

> I do generally get great results, but I don't focus on those in the moment—instead, I just enjoy my task and remain engaged in it alone."

4) Perform with passion: As Dr. Puff's story illustrates, once we are prepared for "the zone," we simply allow ourselves to sink into it and enjoy. Yes, like any skill, this will take practice. We may initially find our minds wandering back to earlier or later today, or even looking for results. That's okay—we can simply return to the moment and perform with passion. Note that this is only possible if we're actually doing something that we are passionate about. It's a whole lot easier to be in "the zone" with things we actually like and have some natural propensity towards. Hence, if we find ourselves unable to sink into "the zone," we may have to stop and ask ourselves whether we have really chosen the right task. The goal is to allow our talents and passions to point us in the right direction…and then just let it flow.

All four of these steps will allow us to cultivate "the zone." By preparing both our skills and our minds, we prep ourselves to be ready for the zone. Then, in the moment, we stop critiquing and stop thinking about results, focusing instead on what is actually before us in that moment. We do it with all the passion we have for the skill or topic, and guess what? It works! Preparing for and cultivating "the zone" in our personal and professional lives is a skill with immense benefits—one certainly worth learning.

Putting It into Practice

In summary, then, "the zone" is a place of increased engagement and confidence. It's a place of peak performance. We can achieve this "high" with a combination of excellence in our craft and presence in the moment. We then experience a number of benefits too, including increased focus, productivity, and results in our professional lives. At the same time, "the zone" allows us to enjoy and engage more fully in our personal lives. In other words, "the zone" is a great place for us to be on all fronts.

And the good news today is that we can intentionally cultivate our ability to be in "the zone." It doesn't have to be something that just sort-of happens on occasion. Instead, we can actually choose to be at our best all of the time. How? Well, we begin with preparation. We become great at what we do, allowing our skills to be so engrained that they are second-nature. Simultaneously, we practice calming our minds so that we can be fully engaged when the time comes to perform. In those performance moments, we are able to fully engage with all of the skill and passion we bring to the table—without critiquing or thinking about any results. These steps may take time, but they also build a skill set of peak performance.

Ready to get started? Well, we've already talked about and practiced the first step of preparing the mind via meditation. We've also talked about choosing a career that builds upon our passion, which hopefully naturally leads us toward the pursuit of excellence. But what about eliminating the judge? Getting our focus off the results, especially in relation to work, can truly be one of the most difficult steps toward being in "the zone."

As a result, we'd like to help you practice taking your focus off results this week. Choose a hobby or activity, preferably one that you do often or really care about. It may be running, golfing, bowling, or anything else. Make it something that you like to excel at, even though the results probably don't make a huge difference in the grand scheme of things. Then go out and do this activity *without keeping track of the results.* If it's golfing or bowling, don't keep score. If it's running, don't time yourself or track your distance. Instead, practice simply being in the moment while you engage in the activity, thinking about your passion instead of your performance. When you're done, return and answer the questions for reflection.

Questions for Reflection

1) What did I learn about being in "the zone" this week?

2) How often do I currently experience "the zone," and is it something I'm doing intentionally?

3) How easy or difficult was it for me to engage in the pure presence of "the zone" with a hobby? Was I able to let go of the results and simply be present and passionate?

4) Based on this activity, and simply my experience in general, what things keep me moving toward or away from "the zone"?

5) Considering what I've read this week and my answers above, what next steps would I like to take toward cultivating "the zone" in my own life?

Tip #18: Be a Limbo Champion

Limbo may be one of the most fun and interesting party games of all time. It's such a basic concept—put some music on and ask people to walk, while bending backwards, under a stick. It almost sounds absurd, yet it really can get the party going. In our experiences of limbo, we've seen three kinds of people: Those who don't really play, those who give it a good effort, and those who win.

Here's what these three players look like: The first group, those who really don't play, either just remain on the sidelines or put in almost zero effort, getting eliminated quite quickly (and usually happily going back to their tables or snacks). The second group, those who give it a good effort, try to make it just under the bar each time, attempting to bend a little lower on each turn. Pretty soon, this group underestimates the placement of the bar, accidentally hitting their stomachs as they start just a little too high, or perhaps bumping their chins as they unbend too soon. Some of the people in this second group are actually quite limber, but they lose because they aren't really warmed up or they are playing too close to the bar. Either way, both the first and second group of limbo players are eliminated sooner or later.

The third group of limbo players, however, ends up victorious. Why? Well, partially because they're limber, of course. But, really, it's also because they are shooting as low as they can go from the very beginning. Unlike the second group, this group doesn't just try to barely make it under the bar. No, this group tends to shoot low every time, often starting out inches or even feet under the pole and keeping their heads all the way back until they've long since cleared it. They are giving it their all and going *way under* the bar right from the very start, which, combined with their limberness, leads them to be victorious in the end.

Interestingly, we see the same three groups of people in the financial arena. Think of the limbo bar as one's financial capacities, or means. The first group doesn't really play or engage; they may enjoy the party, but they care very little about the financial bar, and they end up deeply in debt or some kind of financial trouble rather quickly. The second group puts in some good effort, possibly even trying to maintain a monthly budget, while all the time living just barely at or below the level of the bar…and oftentimes getting eliminated with their own financial troubles eventually as a result. The third group, however, plays all out from the start, shooting low and winning in the end. What does winning look like in the financial arena? Well, probably less debt and more financial security in the long run, plus a whole lot more peace of mind and happiness. Financially, it turns out that it pays to shoot low and live under the bar whenever possible. Although we are not financial advisors, we'll talk in this chapter about what it means to live under the financial bar and how we make this work in our lives.

Recognize the Status Quo

Before we talk about what it means to live under the financial bar, let's flesh out how most of us tend to live now. First of all, we must acknowledge that most of us feel a lot of pressure in this area. We have the pressure of actual needs, like putting food on the table. Plus, we have the pressure from the media and our culture of "keeping up with the Jones's"—or having what our friends and neighbors have. We end up feeling like we "need" the newest gadget, nicest car, or biggest house…why? Really because we are bombarded with ads all day long telling us we'll be happier if we have these things—and, quite frankly, our friends and family do seem pretty excited when they get them. On all sides, we have pressure to go bigger, newer, and shinier.

How do most of us respond to this pressure? Sadly, yet understandably, we play along. Either we throw all caution to the wind, spending outlandishly regardless of our means, or we try to spend as much as possible without quite exceeding our means. We might keep a budget, take out only "good debt," and otherwise try to live just at or below that limbo bar. Forget saving for a rainy day or retirement though, or otherwise getting out of the rat race; instead, we live pretty much paycheck to paycheck, trying to balance our need to stay afloat with "keeping up with the Jones's." Even when we finally get that coveted promotion and raise, we simply use this money to buy more rather than save or pay off our debt. In reality, most of us stretch as far as we can—sometimes within reason and sometimes not—to bend to the pressures around us.

Dr. Puff: "I work in Newport Beach—the capital of go bigger and buy newer. I see people driving the fanciest cars available, wearing extremely expensive designer clothes, and trying to secure the largest estates…whether or not they can afford them. In Newport, these material possessions are all signs of status that only add to the pressure to 'keep up with the Jones's.' However, I see firsthand through my practice what this 'keeping up' does to people—bankruptcy, broken marriages, and simply an immense amount of stress and pressure that prevents people from actually enjoying their day-to-day lives. In the midst of it, I work hard to stay grounded and live within my means. I have nice things, but I don't stretch myself to keep up with others. Instead, I do my best to stick with what's really important to me and keep life fairly simple, even if it means giving up opportunities, making less money, or looking different than others. And the result? I truly enjoy my life every day."

As Dr. Puff's story illustrates, a large majority of people are living in way that tries to keep up with both their needs *and* the culture around them. Unfortunately, most people don't find the mythical happiness they expect by living this way. Yes, we do feel excited when we can purchase the newest smart phone or biggest house. However, this happiness doesn't last. Sooner or later, the stress of keeping up with these purchases catches up with us. It's true: Living at or above the financial bar tends to be pretty stressful. There is very little security in knowing we can probably make it today, but having to worry anytime something happens tomorrow. This is the status quo and, quite frankly, it sucks.

Shoot Below the Bar

Because living at or above the bar tends to be so stressful, we advocate living beneath it. This involves taking the idea of *"living within our means"* to a whole new level. "Living within our means" financially means only purchasing things we have money to pay for now. We don't run up credit card debt for a new car, sweater, or anything else we cannot afford. If we cannot afford to pay even our basic bills, we start to scale down. In other words, we are sure to live at or just barely below the financial bar.

While normal and a step ahead of those who just ignore the bar, it really isn't ideal to live at or barely below the financial bar. The problem is that this way of life commits every dollar we earn, usually to all kinds of both necessary and nice-to-have "stuff." This works great as long as our dollars stay stable. However, we begin to run into real issues when we make less dollars or when life costs a little more. As a result, we advocate taking our finances one step further, like those limbo champions, to shoot way under the bar.

Shooting way under the bar is *living beneath our means.* In this scenario, we can actually pay all of our bills and have money left over for savings or extra expenses. Then, when we run into unexpected car repairs or a pay cut, we're still okay because we have extra money built in to cover these changes. If we live within our means, we might make it, but we will most likely labor under the stress of living paycheck to paycheck. In contrast, living below our means allows us the peace of mind of knowing that we are on top of our finances, even if the unexpected occurs.

Dr. White: "I'm not sure that my husband and I 'live beneath our means' perfectly, but we certainly try. The best example of it for us was finally finishing graduate school. We both finished about the same time and watched our income slowly begin to rise. What did we do with this money? Well, I can tell you it would have been really nice to run out and replace our 30-year-old Diesel car. In reality, however, the car was still running pretty well. We did make some changes, like getting a place with enough room for our expanding family. But we made sure that we still had enough extra money left over to begin rapidly paying down school loans and save for a rainy day. We didn't commit all of our dollars to new expenses. Instead, we tried to live below the bar, paying for necessities and some nice-to-haves, while staying conservative and retaining peace of mind in our commitments."

As Dr. White's story illustrates, living below the bar can sometimes necessitate some hard choices. Perhaps we don't really need that new car or phone right now, even if our friends all have one. Ideally, we keep things simple; if we get extra opportunities or stuff, fantastic! But we allow these extra toys to be the icing on the cake rather than making them a level of necessity we are constantly trying to keep up with. This is what it means to live beneath our means.

Make It a Reality

So how do we make "living beneath our means" a reality? Well, more than anything else, it's probably a change of mindset. We shift from thinking we "must" have all of the latest toys, gadgets, etc. to realizing we are already pretty blessed with what we do have. We focus on enjoying what really matters in our lives (which is often non-material things, like our families) and allow the "stuff" to come with time. Having said that, here are some specific mind and action changes to consider:

~Budget: That's right—we used the "b" word! If we want to be truly victorious in our finances, we have to create a solid plan and stick to it. We'll talk more about how to do this in the exercise for this week. Suffice it to say now, financial success will not just happen. And, no, it's not simply a matter of making more money; if this was the case, we wouldn't have movie stars and others who have struck it big financially and then go bankrupt later in their lives. Financial success involves actually planning with discernment and executing with discipline, starting with a budget (and possibly adding more complicated financial statements later).

~Pay ourselves first: As we budget, it's important to pay ourselves first. This means that we allocate a certain percentage of money to savings or other rainy day categories. If we instead wait to see what money is left

over at the end of the month, there will almost never be enough for savings. Just as our activities seem to expand to fill the time we have, our expenses seem to expand to fill the money we have. As a result, we must set aside a certain dollar amount or percentage for savings (specifically how much is up to you and your financial planner) in our budget and bank accounts before allocating money to all of our expenses.

~Prioritize: When it comes to expenses, it's critical to prioritize. We cannot afford every nice-to-have now, even if everyone around us seems to somehow find the money for these items. (As a side note, don't be thrown off by what other people have as they may be in limbo groups 1 or 2, spending what they can't afford and heading for financial disaster.) So the question becomes, what is really most important to me and my family? Is it the nicer car, newer gadget, or bigger house? What really matters to us…as opposed to being just another example of "keeping up with the Jones's"? The answers to this question will direct us in how to prioritize expenses for the money we do have.

~Spend wisely: In addition to prioritizing our spending, we can make our money go farther by spending wisely. Perhaps we can take advantage of free or discounted opportunities in a multitude of ways. This may include anything from exchanging free babysitting with a friend to utilizing coupons or online deals for the things we really want. Maybe it even involves learning to take advantage of free things that are fun, like hiking, the beach, or that one day per month that's free at the local

museum. In other words, it behooves us to make our money go as far as possible by spending what we do have wisely.

~Increase savings and other assets: As our income increases (or we're even able to lower our expenses by prioritizing—yippee!), it's important that we don't just take on new expenses for every "extra" dollar. It is very common that a raise at work means we go out and buy a nicer car or a bigger home. Although it is great to celebrate our successes and there's nothing wrong with having nice things, this behavior becomes a problem when it simply keeps raising the bar of bare necessity such that we are always just keeping up with our expenses…or, worse yet, getting further and further behind as we take out more loans to buy that new car or bigger house. Part of living beneath our means involves allocating our "extra" dollars to increase savings or other assets as much or more to pay for new expenses.

~Pay off—or, better yet, avoid—debt: In addition to saving money, it's often a good idea to pay off our debt as quickly as possible. While the bank will give us 25-30 years to pay for our mortgage or school loans, this actually benefits them more than us. Why? Because we end up paying way more for the house, education, car, or other item in interest. Paying off these debts sooner will benefit us by actually putting more money in our pockets in the long-run. Although it's outside the scope of this chapter to elaborate fully, let us also say that it likewise behooves us to keep our debt as minimal as possible. Some people will say we should avoid all debt, while

others will say there are some kinds of debt that are "good" (e.g., school loans, mortgage). We'll say this: Is it *really* necessary to take out debt for that item? Could we, for example, buy a used or simply cheaper, new car that we have the cash for, instead of buying the more expensive one that requires a loan? Yes, it may be an uncommon or even unpopular decision to avoid debt or pay it off quickly, but again, it puts more money (and a whole lot less stress) in our pockets in the long-run.

~Find like-minded people: As we make these difficult financial choices, it helps to have like-minded people in our lives. We've talked about this before in relation to all kinds of things—from food and exercise to the way we think. It's true here too: The people around us matter. It's easier to make wise, even if uncommon decisions, when our friends and family are making similar decisions. Conversely, it's much harder to buy the used car without a loan or save the money from our promotion when we are the only ones taking this route. Finding and befriending other people who want to live beneath the bar will help us stay on-track (and feel less crazy!) about our own decisions.

~Remember, we are more than our money! Lastly, let us add one theoretical, yet quite important, reminder: We are more than our money and our possessions. In fact, we are not defined by the job title we hold, the income we make, the numbers in our budget, the car we drive, or even the brand we wear. Other people will sometimes see these things as status symbols and seek to define us by them. Fortunately, the labels only stick if we

let them. We can choose to define ourselves instead by other things, like the meaning in our lives, the happiness we experience with our families and friends, or the inner peace we find by living a holistically balanced and healthy life.

The truth is, in spite of everything our culture has told us, money and possessions really don't buy happiness. If anything, happiness is much more likely to come from living beneath our means. Why? Because then our lives don't revolve around money. We can spend our energy and time thinking about, pursuing, and enjoying other things in life. Yes, living beneath our means involves making hard choices that keep our debt and financial commitments to a minimum and our savings and other assets at a maximum. There are a number of tools we can use to aid us in the process, such as keeping a budget, paying ourselves first, prioritizing our expenses, spending wisely, and finding like-minded people. In the end, though, it is really a choice we make: What will we allow ourselves to drive and define us? Will it be money or something else entirely?

Putting It into Practice

The joy of living below the bar is that our lives don't have to revolve around money. Yes, money matters. We need it to pay for our bills and take our families on vacation. We can't get around that fact. However, we can do a lot to decide whether this reality will be consuming and stressful in our lives, or just one more detail to balance. In order to accomplish the latter, we advocate living below our means.

Living below our means differs from the status quo. It means that we pay attention to our finances, but not in a way that allows us to spend as much as possible without going bankrupt. Instead, we shoot to spend significantly under our means, enabling us to maximize assets and minimize debts. This often involves some hard choices that force us to prioritize what really matters to us rather than what "the Jones's" or others care about. Nonetheless, it allows us to achieve peace of mind and (usually) much greater financial success in the long-run. In other words, by shooting low, we become like those limbo champions who play all out and end up victorious.

The best place to start in all of this is by taking a look at our current budgets and our spending. Specifically, complete the worksheet below by following these three steps:

Step 1 – "Current Budget": If you already have a budget, pull it out and use it to complete the first column in the worksheet below. If you don't have a budget, feel free to quickly jot down what you imagine that you spend on a monthly basis in this column.

Step 2 – "Actual Spending": Next, grab last month's credit card bills and bank statements to help you complete the "actual spending" column. Note that a 3-6 month average would be most ideal here, but one month will suffice to get you started. Either way, make sure to consider quarterly or annual expenses (e.g., car registration, property taxes) and divide them out to be monthly so that you can include them in this column too.

Try to account for all of your expenses, even adding categories as needed.

Step 3 – "New Budget": Lastly, take some time to evaluate your current budget (or perceived spending) compared to your actual spending. You can use the questions at the end of this chapter to get you thinking. Also, consider what you've read. Are you, for example, increasing your savings/assets each month or barely scraping by on each paycheck? Incorporate any changes you'd like to make into your "new budget."

Note that completing this worksheet will take you some time. At some point, it may also involve the help of others, such as a friend who's good with numbers, a spouse, or a financial planner. Don't let that deter you! This activity is absolutely worth the time and help required because of what it will contribute to your financial health and peace of mind in the end. When you've completed the worksheet, answer the questions below if you haven't already done so.

	Current Budget	Actual Spending	New Budget
Income:			
Income from work			
Income from assets (e.g., rental property)			
Other income			
TOTAL INCOME			

	Current Budget	Actual Spending	New Budget
Expenses:			
Taxes			
Savings			
Investments (e.g., retirement)			
Giving			
Mortgage/rent			
Utilities (e.g., gas, water, electricity)			
Property taxes			
Cell phone			
Car payment			
Car insurance			
Car registration			
Misc car (e.g., repairs, AAA, wash, parking)			
Gas			
Travel (e.g., plane, bus, hotel)			
Groceries/toiletries			
Food out			
Entertainment			
Media (e.g., books, magazines, CDs)			
Clothing			
Hair & nails			
Gym			
Personal services (e.g. massage, therapy)			
Childcare			
Insurance (e.g., medical, life)			
Medical/dental			

	Current Budget	Actual Spending	New Budget
Professional expenses (e.g., accounting)			
School tuition/loans			
Credit card debt			
Other: ____________			
Other: ____________			
Other: ____________			
TOTAL EXPENSES			
SURPLUS (i.e., income – expenses)			

Questions for Reflection

1) How is my actual spending the same or different than my budget, or perceived spending? What surprised me most here?

2) Do my budget and spending equate to living above, at, or below the financial bar? How do my assets, debts, and/or peace of mind reflect my experience in this particular "limbo" group?

3) What steps would I like to take (e.g., paying myself first, prioritizing my spending) in order to live below (or simply further below) the bar? How can I make these changes in my budget, *and* make sure they get integrated into my actual spending? What will I do with these "extra" dollars (e.g., pay off debt faster, save, invest in assets)?

4) What feelings will these changes bring up about my status or worth (for myself or important others)?

5) Is there anyone in my life who is like-minded and can help me make (or simply stick to) some of these hard choices?

Tying It All Together

In this section, we've talked about how we can thrive in our professional lives. First, how do we find satisfaction and even success in our careers? Ideally, we follow the pleasure principle into finding work that we enjoy. We might enjoy the activity itself or the meaning it provides for us. Either way, we also orchestrate all the little details of our career, ranging from scheduling to environment, to make our days more positive and life-giving for us. We control what we can and let go of what we can't, thus *following the pleasure principle* into greater enjoyment of just about any job or career.

In addition to enjoying our jobs, we also want to make them a place of confidence and productivity. We want to experience greater results in terms of both the quantity and quality of our work. These components allow our work to flourish; they also create more satisfaction in our lives overall. How do we accomplish all this? We build our skills to excellence and then learn to be fully present in the moment—a winning combination that allows us to *get in the zone* and achieve peak performance while we work.

By finding ways to enjoy and thrive in our work, we're likely to find more success both personally and professionally. Hopefully, we'll even thrive financially as a result. In reality, though, no matter how much money we make, we have to manage it well in order to take care of our needs and wants in life without tons of stress. Specifically, we advocate "living below the bar" in terms of our finances, or regularly spending less than our means. This may differ from the status quo and involve some hard choices and prioritizing. Still, it's worth both the peace of mind and typical, long-term financial payoff it provides for us. In other words, by shooting low, we get to *be limbo champions* who play all out and end up victorious.

Although not exhaustive, these three steps will allow us pleasure, success, and peace of mind in our work and finances. These areas will become ones that feed us (literally and figuratively!) rather than starve us. Not only will that make work more enjoyable, it'll actually allow us more energy and mental space to enjoy our personal lives too. Hence, like those professional dancers, we can actually find ways to make the "work" of life a place of pleasure and thriving too.

Conclusion

We hope you've enjoyed "dancing" with us through this book. In truth, it's been quite a journey! We've covered a lot of ground, including everything from the mind, heart, and body to relationships, work, and finances. Why so much? Because we believe that a lot of success in life comes through a holistic focus.

As a dancer, there are many pieces to this holistic focus. First, it's important to do the work to learn the steps and develop excellence. At the same time, a dancer must keep his/her body in shape—ideally through a mix of discipline and fun. And, of course, the dancer must do all of this without losing heart or focus; in other words, he/she must hold on to a passion for the dance *in the present moment* in order to really infuse it with beauty and life. In almost all cases, the dancer must be able to do this with others too—really coordinating steps with grace and ease. All of these pieces are important for the dancer, emphasizing a holistic focus that takes in all aspects of the dance.

Similarly for us, it's important to attend to all the most central areas of life in order to really achieve lasting success, happiness, and more. It truly is a fallacy that we can just attend to one area and have everything work out okay in the end. Being a workaholic or even a one-dimensional stay-at-home mom, for example, will cost us in the long-run. Like a dancer, it behooves us to attend to all the central areas of life; some of these are internal, like our heart, mind, and body, while others are external, like work, finances, and relationships. A holistic focus that attends to all of these central areas is critical.

Remember the Benefits of Dancing

The good news, though, is that a holistic focus does not have to be overwhelming or painful. It is not one of those things, like brussel sprouts or liver, that are good for us in an icky, barely tolerable, kind of way. In other words, it is not good for us in the way that we'll hate every minute of it even though we know we need to do it. There are parts of holistic health, like skill and discipline, that take intentionality and effort similar to that of the master or professional dancer. There are just as many, however, like passion and presence, that are best modeled by the carefree child. Holistic health is a new way of living that combines the skill of the master and the abandon of the child to empower us to be great and enjoy life as it is.

Hopefully, you've long since begun to see the benefits of a holistic focus in your life. Just in case there are any who are still skeptical, however, perhaps wanting to jettison an area or two that don't feel quite as essential (or easy), consider the following: *Research* has shown a number of benefits from holistic health. As we take a more in-depth look, we see specifically that holistic health has been shown to be helpful in a number of ways, including:

- Preventing or improving illness;
- Reducing anxiety and stress;

- Decreasing our feelings of guilt and negative thinking;
- Improving our ability to relax;
- Providing a greater sense of connection to ourselves and others;
- Enabling us to experience greater creativity and problem-solving abilities;
- Increasing our hope, peace, sense of empowerment, and overall well-being.

That's a lot!! Truly, it turns out that just as holistic health engages our physical, emotional, cognitive, professional, and relational health, it has the potential to benefit us in all of these areas too. [xxi, xxii, xxiii, xxiv, xxv, xxvi, xxvii] Holistic health is an incredibly powerful strategy for dancing through life.

Don't Stop Dancing!

We share all of these benefits now because we know that holistic health is not something we can read one book about and be done with. Holistic health is a lifestyle, and we want to continue to ignite your excitement for it, even as this book comes to a close. We hope that hearing all of these benefits just makes you increasingly motivated to work toward positive changes in your life—while, of course, enjoying the process along the way!

There are a number of ways you can continue moving toward holistic health. First of all, it's important to celebrate the ways you've already grown, as enjoying where we are at now is a major component of holistic health. Second, you might want to set small, achievable, and specific goals. It's helpful to focus on one thing at a time. It's also important to stick with this area for a month or more in order to actually begin establishing new habits. Third, it might be helpful to set up a regular coffee or walk with a like-minded person who can provide some community and accountability in this area. A fourth option is to sign up for our newsletters on our websites (www.kristenmwhite.com and www.doctorpuff.com) to see what else we can add to your journey. Fifth, and most importantly, it's essential to simply have grace with yourself in moving through this journey, as criticism and judgment get us nowhere. Overall, there are truly many ways we can work toward a more positive life while also enjoying the one we have.

As we do this, of course, we begin to experience more and more holistic success, replacing our two left feet with the spontaneity of a child and skill of a master. This is surely the way to dance through life—trading the laborious, boring, and stressful ways we often move between alarm clocks with the ease and grace that come with combining great skill and the freedom and abandon of a free-spirited child. As you improve your skill, we hope that you are indeed able to enjoy the process, looking great and getting fantastic results. Enjoy, and keep dancing!

About the Authors

Dr. Robert Puff is a clinical psychologist, author, consultant, speaker, and coach, who has been successfully helping individuals, families, organizations, and businesses for over 20 years. Dr. Puff is the author of numerous books, including *Anger Work: How To Express Your Anger and Still Be Kind, Living a Peaceful Life, How To Live a Positive Life, Success Beyond Your Imagination*, and *Meditation for Health and Happiness.* He is the co-author and co-creator of *Raising Healthy Children and Teenagers* and *Getting It Right: A Guide to Healthy Relationships.*

Dr. Puff has a Masters degree from Princeton as well as both a second Masters degree and a Ph.D. in clinical psychology from Fuller. He taught as an adjunct professor at Rosemead Graduate School of Psychology. Over the years, he has been on staff at Trenton Psychiatric Hospital, Sepulveda V.A. Medical Hospital, La Puente Mental Health, and St. Judes Medical Hospital.

In the past several years, Dr. Puff has given over a thousand media interviews, including magazines, online magazines, TV, and radio talk shows. He has consulted with businesses and organizations. People seek his expertise on various psychological and business topics including: personal and work relationship issues, depression, parenting, stress and anger management, meditation, healing from past traumas, holistic success, and "In the Zone" selling and management.

Dr. Puff works with businesses and organizations as a speaker and coach. To learn more about Dr. Puff and his numerous works on holistic success, visit his website: www.DoctorPuff.com.

Kristen M. White, Psy.D. is a clinical psychologist who is passionate about creating positive, healthy relationships. She recognizes that many people do not have the knowledge, skills, or history to easily experience such relationships with themselves or others on a day-to-day basis. Instead, they end up experiencing significant anguish and difficulty intrapersonally (e.g., depression, anxiety) as well as interpersonally (e.g., isolation, divorce). Consequently, Dr. White desires to come alongside others, both inside and outside of the therapy office, helping them to make the transformative and life-giving power of emotions and relationships a reality in their own lives.

Dr. White received her Masters and Doctoral degrees in Clinical Psychology from Rosemead School of Psychology in La Mirada, CA. She completed her Bachelor's degree in Philosophy & Theology with a minor in Psychology at Point Loma University in San Diego. Dr. White currently works as a therapist, professor, speaker, writer, and consultant. In all of these settings, she strives to use her knowledge, expertise, and personal experience to assist others in increasing their emotional and relational intelligence in all aspects of their lives. For more information on Dr. White, her publications, and services, visit her website at www.kristenmwhite.com.

References

[i] Bacon, L. (2008). *Health at Every Size: The Surprising Truth About Your Weight.* Dallas: Benbella Books, Inc.
[ii] Nelson, C. (2009). Appreciating gratitude: Can gratitude be used as a psychological intervention to improve individual well-being? *Counseling Psychology Review, 24,* 38-50.
[iii] Chan, D. W. (2010). Gratitude, gratitude intervention and subjective well-being among Chinese school teachers in Hong Kong. *Educational Psychology, 30,* 139-153.
[iv] Wood, A. M. (2008). The role of gratitude in the development of social support, stress, and depression: Two longitudinal studies. *Journal of Research in Personality, 42,* 854-871.
[v] American Academy of Sleep Medicine (2009). Meditatio may be an effective treatment for insomnia. *ScienceDaily.* Retrieved June 15, 2009 from http://www.sciencedaily.com/releases/2009/06/090609072719.htm.
[vi] Eksteins, A. (2010). Meditation may be the future of anti-aging. *Naturalnews.com.*
[vii] Krasner, M. S., Epstein, R. M., Beckman, H., Suchman, A. L., Chapman, B., Mooney, C. J., Quill, T. E. (2009). Association of an educational program in mindful communication with burnout, empathy, and attitudes among primary care physicians. *The Journal of the American Medical Association, 302.* Retrieved October 17, 2009 from http://jama.ama-assn.org/cgi/content/abstract/302/12/1284.
[viii] Wake Forest Baptist Medical Center. (2011). Demystifying meditation: Brain imagine illustrates how meditation reduces pain. *ScienceDaily.* Retrieved April 11, 2011, from

http://www.sciencedaily.com/releases/2011/04/110405174835.htm.
[ix] Broyd, N. (2010). Meditation not medication for depression. *WebMD.com.* Retrieved from http://www.webmd.boots.com/depression/news/20100106/meditation-not-medication-for-depression.
[x] Massachusetts General Hospital. (2011). Meditation may help the brain 'turn down the volume on distractions. *ScienceDaily.* Retrieved May 3, 2011 from http://www.sciencedaily.com/releases/2011/04/110421122337.htm.
[xi] Doheny, K. (2010). Can meditation reverse memory loss? *WebMD.* Retrieved from http://www.webmd.com/alzheimers/news/20100303/can-meditation-reverse-memory-loss?src=RSS_PUBLIC.
[xii] Condor, B. (2009). Meditate to melt stress, improve health. *Chicagotribune.com.* Retrieved from www.chicagotribune.com/health/chi-tc-health-action-breathe-112.ar0nov29,0,4526770.story.
[xiii] Hotting, K., Reich, B., Holzschneider, K., Kauschke, K., Schmidt, T., Reer, R., Braumann, K-M., & Roder, B. (2011). Differential cognitive effects of cycling versus stretching/coordination training in middle-aged adults. *Health Psychology, Online First Publication,* 1-11.
[xiv] King, A. C., Taylor, C. B., & Haskett, W. L. (1993). Effects of differing intensities and formats of 12 months of exercise training on psychological outcomes in older adults. *Health Psychology, 12,* 292-300.
[xv] Hansen, C. J., Stevens, L. C., & Coast, R. (2001). Exercise duration and mood state: How much is enough to feel better? *Health Psychology, 20,* 267-275.
[xvi] Wilfley, D., & Kunce, J. (1986). Differential physical and psychological effects of exercise. *Journal of Counseling Psychology, 33,* 337-342.
[xvii] Norvell, N., & Belles, D. (1993). Psychological and physical benefits of circuit weight training in law

enforcement personnel. *Journal of Consulting and Clinical Psychology, 61,* 520-527.
[xviii] Davis, C. L., Tomprowski, P. D., McDowell, J. E., Austin, B. P., Miller, P. H., Yanasak, N. E., Allison, J. D., & Naglieri, J. A. (2011). Exercise improves executive function and achievement and alters brain activation in overweight children: A randomized, controlled trial. *Health Psychology, 30,* 91-98.
[xix] Bacon, L. (2008). *Health at Every Size: The Surprising Truth About Your Weight.* Dallas: Benbella Books, Inc.
[xx] Amen, D. G. (2010). *Change Your Brain, Change Your Body: Use Your Brain to Get and Keep the Body You Have Always Wanted.* Harmony Books: New York.
[xxi] Liu, C. J., Hsiung, P. C., Change, K. J., Chang, K. J., Liu, Y. F., Wang, K. C., Hsiao, S. M. N., & Chan, C. L. W. (2008). A study on the efficacy of body-mind spirit group therapy for patients with breast cancer. *Journal of Clinical Nursing, 17,* 2539-2549.
[xxii] Ho, R. T. H., Potash, J..S., Fu, W., Wong, K. P. L., & Chan, C. L. W. (2010). Changes in breast cancer patients after psychosocial intervention as indicated in drawings. *Psycho-Oncology, 19,* 353-360.
[xxiii] Chan, C. L. W., Ng, S. M., Ho, R. T. H., & Chow, A. Y. M. (2006). East meets West: Applying Eastern spirituality in clinical practice. *Journal of Clinical Nursing, 15,* 822-832.
[xxiv] Chan, C. L. W., Chan, Y., & Lou, V. W. Q. (2002). Evaluating an empowerment group for divorced Chinese women in Hong Kong. *Research on Social Work Practice, 12,* 558-569.
[xxv] Stefan, S., & Brucklacher, M. A. (1984). Putting the pieces back into the whole: An experiential course on holistic health. *Teaching of Psychology, 11,* 117-118.
[xxvi] Higgins, S. J. W., Lauzon, L. L., Yew, A. C., Bratseth, C. D., & McLeod, N. (2010). Wellness 101: Health education for the university student. *Health Education, 110,* 309-327.

[xxvii] Crawford, A. M. (2000). An integration of mind/body medicine and the expressive arts therapies. *Dissertation Abstracts International: Section B: The Sciences and Engineering, 60,* 5238.

8689165R00172

Made in the USA
San Bernardino, CA
20 February 2014